The Teaching Voice

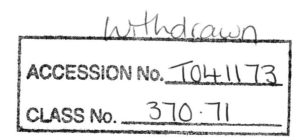

Stephanie Martin and Lyn Darnley

The Teaching Voice

Stephanie Martin and Lyn Darnley

Whurr Publishers Ltd
London

© 1996 Whurr Publishers and The British Voice Association
First published 1996
Whurr Publishers Ltd
19B Compton Terrace, London N1 2UN, England

Reprinted 1997 and 1999

British Library Cataloguing-in-Publication Data
A catalogue record for this book is available from the
British Library.

ISBN 1-897635-19-2

Printed and bound in the UK by Athenaeum Press Ltd,
Gateshead, Tyne & Wear

Contents

Preface

This book was written in response to requests from teachers for information about the theory and practice of the voice; information that many regretted they had not had access to during their professional training.

It is for all those who use the voice for the purposes of teaching or informing. It aims principally to address the needs of student teachers and teachers in infant, primary and secondary schools and to be of use to lecturers in the college and university sectors; dance, drama and sports instructors; public speakers in professions such as the clergy and the law; and those in commerce and industry whose professions require communication that is heavily dependent on the voice.

The authors, a speech and language therapist and a voice teacher, ran joint workshops for teachers experiencing vocal difficulties. Organised by the British Voice Association with the financial support of the Inchape Foundation, workshops were held over a period of seven years and repeatedly the requests from participants were the same. What was wanted was a book that answered a multitude of needs; to offer detailed information on voice care and on the physiology of voice, while at the same time supplying practical advice on aspects of delivery, communication skills and classroom strategies, which would be supported by exercises for developing the resonance, range and projection of the voice.

The authors recognise that the needs of individuals differ widely, consequently some information will be particularly useful for some individuals and less useful for others. The aim of this book is to offer a mix of practice and theory, which will allow teachers and professional voice users to understand how the voice works, to explore some of the factors that influence voice production and most importantly, to offer readers strategies and solutions which will provide a framework to keep them in good voice throughout their professional career. It is not however a substitute for practical teaching which is fundamental to a profession that involves extensive voice use.

This book is dedicated to the teachers who asked the questions and who provide a function that is one of the most important in our society.

Acknowledgements

Special thanks to:-
Brian Darnley, Rob Day, Jane Dobson, Wendy Greenhill, Geraldine Judd, Peter Martin, Glyn MacDonald, Mo Pattimore, Shelley Sawers, Heather Steed, Steve Tasker and Tessa Vale
and to the following organisations :-
The British Voice Association, The London Institute of Education, Rose Bruford College and The Royal Shakespeare Company

About the authors

Stephanie Martin is an arts graduate from the Open University who qualified as a speech and language therapist from the Central School of Speech and Drama London, and completed a post graduate year at the University of Georgia. She has a Masters degree in Voice Studies.

She has combined clinical practice with research and currently teaches on the BSc (Hons) Clinical Communication Sciences degree and the Post Graduate Diploma in Voice Studies at the Central School. In addition she is a Senior Commissioning Editor for Winslow. She has had articles published in journals and periodicals and her *Working with Dysphonics* and *Voice Exemplified* are published by Winslow.

Lyn Darnley is a voice teacher with dual teaching qualifications from Trinity College London and the University of South Africa and a Masters degree from the University of Birmingham. Her professional background includes working as a performer and voice coach in theatre, television and radio and in schools as a specialist teacher.

Before joining The Royal Shakespeare Company as a Voice Coach she spent twelve years at the Rose Bruford College of Speech and Drama on the Community Theatre and BA (Hons) Acting Courses and for eight of those years was Head of Voice.

Both authors were members of The British Voice Association's working party on the Care and Development of the Teacher's Voice and gave regular joint workshops in the London area.

Their interest in the teaching voice has taken them to many European countries, the United States and South Africa. Previous joint publications have included articles for journals and periodicals. Their previous publication *The Voice Sourcebook* (Winslow 1992) offers a unique perspective on voice as seen from both disciplines.

Chapter 1
The Teacher's Voice

The Teacher as a Professional Voice User

The teacher in company with the lecturer, the politician, the telephonist, the radio announcer, the vicar and the actor can be said to fall within the category of professional voice user.

The use of the word 'professional' carries with it an expectation that the individual has some expertise in a particular area, at one end of the continuum the individual would be expected to exhibit more than basic skill in the named area, and at the other end of the continuum one would confidently anticipate that the individual would have had training to raise their ability to a level significantly higher than that of the average person.

Therefore this categorisation of professional voice user would suggest someone who is skilled at using their voice, who has a professional training to support prolonged use of their voice in difficult situations and has an ability to use their voice effectively in a variety of settings and to differing groups and numbers of people.

Teacher Training Provision

When we refer to teachers as professional voice users we are attributing this term to them in respect of the amount of time during their working day that the teacher has to spend talking. It is an undisputed fact that for most teachers any voice work during their teacher training is minimal, if not non-existent, and certainly provision for voice training remains on an ad hoc basis in most training establishments. Voice training, if offered, can range from a non-compulsory hour's talk to, at the most, a half day of practical work, with proportionately few students in training ever having an opportunity for more than this.

It would seem that within the many subject areas that are deemed essential for teachers to master before they can be said to have qualified to teach, the effective use of voice is so low on the list as to be non-existent with only a few notable exceptions.

In a survey of teachers, 93% of teachers questioned regarded their voice as an important professional tool and yet of those questioned only 16% had had any practical work on their own voice during training (Martin 1994). When we look more closely at this sample, many of those teachers who had had some training qualified several years ago when more time was given to voice work. With the popular Post Graduate Certificate of Education (PGCE), time is even more pressured and trainee teachers have even less opportunity to develop vocal skills. The period of training for the PGCE is only a year, and in fact some student teachers go out into the schools only two weeks after the beginning of term. One student we spoke to had been given one group voice class lasting an hour and this was offered in the middle of the period of training. This method of 'into the fire' apprenticeship has its merits perhaps, but these unfortunately do not lie in the area of the prospective teacher's vocal health, neither do they offer the children the advantage of a teacher who is at ease vocally. When the voice is under stress it loses the nuance and subtlety that enhances delivery and adds to the child's experience of learning.

Vocal Requirements for Teaching

If teachers are to teach effectively the undisputed fact is that they need voices which are able to withstand the demands of prolonged voice use seven hours a day, five days a week and for up to twelve to sixteen weeks a term. There is no question that for all but the most garrulous individual to spend this amount of time talking would be almost inconceivable. Most non-professional voice users readily acknowledge the effects of any unexpected or prolonged voice use; saying they feel tired, often their throat feels sore and their voice is less than reliable.

It should of course be possible to use the voice without tiring, damaging or abusing it for prolonged periods of time, but that presupposes that the conditions under which one is using the voice are ideal. Among these conditions would be that the individual is physiologically sound, mentally alert, emotionally untroubled and in a friendly, supportive and comfortable environment. It is hardly necessary to say that for the majority of teachers only a few of these factors will prevail at any one time.

Few if any teachers work in ideal conditions. Ideal conditions in terms of physical space would be acoustically balanced, warm but not overheated, well-ventilated buildings. In addition, few (if any) teachers are able to produce voice in an easy and relaxed manner, with well-balanced posture, good control of breath and minimal mental stress. That is not in any way to 'blame' the teacher but simply to take a realistic look at the conditions that currently prevail within the teaching profession and to recognise how difficult it is for teachers to expect to be able to fulfil any of the above 'ideal' criteria.

The Classroom Setting

In the classroom setting the teacher needs to be prepared to speak for a large part of every lesson. Primary school teachers particularly need to use their voices at a level which can be heard above a steady hum of background noise. Current thinking in education is to encourage children to verbalise ideas and explore language, so that they use speech to explore their world and develop their social and personal skills. Four- and five-year-old children are not able, for the most part, to sustain long periods without talking, and indeed few within the profession would advocate a return to the much more rigid 'silence is golden' philosophy of previous years. It does however create difficulties particularly for the primary school teacher, in terms of voice conservation, as there are few periods in the day when the teacher is guaranteed silence and it is therefore most important that the teacher develops strategies to maximise opportunities for easy voicing.

The teacher who has completed a one year Post Graduate Certificate of Education course where classroom practice is fairly concentrated, is often at more of a disadvantage than those teachers who have been eased gradually into the classroom environment during a four-year training period. These teachers often find it is difficult to assess the degree of vocal effort needed to make themselves heard over a particular level of background noise and this can lead to early episodes of vocal strain. An unfortunate consequence of vocal strain early on in one's professional life is that while periods of vocal rest away from school will help to ease the problem (which is why teachers often report that half-term breaks and holiday periods help to alleviate the symptoms) once a pattern has been established it is difficult for the teacher to alter their method of talking without help. Help from an outside agency once the teacher begins to work and to experience difficulties may be difficult to access or arrange, which is why training prior to the teacher going into the classroom is so essential. Chapters 8 and 9 explore strategies for dealing with many of the vocally demanding aspects of teaching.

Classroom Design

Even when background noise is not a problem, classroom design is often ill thought out in terms of the demands it places on the teacher's voice. New schools are built to encourage openness, which is invaluable in terms of the school functioning as a community, but it is much more difficult to use the voice effectively in large open spaces, where there are problems of poor acoustics and the dampening or absorption of sound due to the building materials used. Working in new purpose-built high-tech schools with lots of glass, exposed brickwork and open spaces is often just as demanding vocally as working in older schools. Older schools, which range from those housed in their original 19th century buildings with cathedral roofs, to the 1960's glass and concrete structures so beloved of new town planners, all have their own problems acoustically and environmentally and these should not be overlooked.

Ergonomics

An additional factor which teachers often fail to take into consideration is that classrooms are principally arranged to accommodate the needs of the pupils, rather than providing for the vocal needs of the teacher. In the infant and primary classes children sit on small chairs around small tables: a seating plan which is supposed to encourage conversation and to give the small child security and a feeling of being at home in a friendly environment. This is obviously essential for children, but apart from offering unlimited opportunities to chat and therefore increase the level of background noise over which the teacher has to speak, it also presents the teacher with problems in terms of ergonomics. The height of the tables means that the teacher has either to crouch by the side of the table or bend over, in order to make eye contact when talking to the pupils. Later chapters give more information on the anatomy and structure of the larynx and how the voice is affected both directly and indirectly by postural changes, but it is important to stress at this point that bending awkwardly and vocalising at the same time is not conducive to easy voicing. Crouching is more vocally desirable but possibly less dignified; also, crouching or bending at the knee requires much more conscious effort on the part of the teacher, who on spontaneously responding to a pupil will instinctively tend to bend rather than to crouch with concomitant strain on back, neck and ultimately the voice.

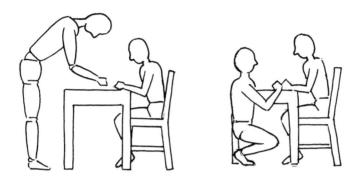

Figure 1: *Incorrect position*   **Figure 2:** *Correct position*

Actors who are required to perform in physically limiting positions would generally insist on being taught the necessary physical and vocal techniques in order to prevent vocal strain, if necessary involving the support of their union. Why does the same not apply to the teaching profession? The answer regrettably is that there has been little or no recognition of the vocal demands of teaching and a gross underestimation of the need to train the teacher's voice. Commerce, industry and politics acknowledge the benefit of training in voice and communication skills, so why is the teacher still overlooked?

One reason must be that within the teaching profession there appears to be a tacit acceptance that voice problems 'come with the territory': if you teach you must expect to have voice problems. The received wisdom seems to be that these will occur with more or less frequency and be of greater or lesser severity according to 'luck'. You are lucky if you get through a term without a problem. In fact there is no scientific proof that luck plays any part in the maintenance of good voice, but what is undisputed is the fact that, with adequate voice training, most teachers would be able to sustain voice with little effort during prolonged periods of teaching.

Additional Factors Affecting Voice

An additional factor which teachers often fail to take account of are the extra duties that they have to undertake. Many teachers feel pressured to be seen to play a full and active part in the school and consequently find themselves taking responsibility for after-school clubs, activities and sporting fixtures. One junior school known to the authors has thirty-five after-school activities on offer to pupils and this school is not an exception. It would be interesting to consider the additional stress this places on the teacher, when to not volunteer for additional extracurricular activities is tantamount to signalling that you have no interest in promotion or advancement within the profession.

Responsibilities such as playground duty will mean that many teachers end up shouting to gain attention out of doors in all weather, above the noise of playing or fighting children. Similarly with sports activities, where children are generally noisy and very excited, teachers often have no other recourse than to shout when trying to gain their attention. Shouting under stress, unless done properly through a learned technique, is potentially very vocally abusive and allied to this are the problems of different weather conditions. Teachers have to go out to supervise children in cold, misty weather and then return inside to generally overheated and poorly ventilated school buildings.

Sports classes held inside in a gym with little ventilation are also full of vocal 'minefields', but possibly the most difficult situation of all is where a teacher has to supervise pupils in echoing swimming pools. One teacher remarked that her voice had never been the same since she started to teach groups of pupils swimming at a municipal baths. She simply tried to shout louder to make herself heard and ended up experiencing quite severe vocal strain. While there is an acceptance that certain extracurricular activities do require special skills and allowances are given, there are very few occasions on which recommendations are made regarding the vocal skills required. Drama classes, music and singing classes also form part of the primary teacher's role and indeed music is an essential component of teaching within the primary school. There is no question that these activities should be omitted but it is important to recognise that many teachers have had no proper training, indeed some simply acquire these skills in an ad hoc manner as a result of their teaching experience. For many teachers without proper singing or voice training, these activities prove to be too much and their voices break down, sometimes resulting in the need to change profession. A common complaint of many teachers is that, 'I used to be able to sing but now I simply cannot do more than guide and monitor my pupils, and as for my singing range, it has reduced dramatically.'

This statement or one conveying the same message can be heard frequently when working with teachers. What is perhaps the most extraordinary aspect of it is the calm acceptance that this is a common aspect of the job – your voice goes, or at the very least your vocal range diminishes.

In the United Kingdom the issue of repetitive strain injury (RSI) has enjoyed considerable media attention and indeed has been proved to be a painful and distressing side effect for many workers, notably among women who had worked over a period of several years for a large telephone and communications system in the United Kingdom. Those who had suffered RSI and could prove that this had occurred as a function of their working life were awarded substantial sums for damages. What is the difference between the repetitive strain injuries exhibited by the vocal folds of hundreds of teachers (which leave them with inadequately functioning voices) and the repetitive strain injuries experienced by those communication workers? The difference appears to lie in the lack of importance we have historically ascribed to voice problems, not only in the United Kingdom but worldwide. The low priority given to voice training for teachers, the shortsightedness of the approach by education authorities and training establishments, means that many hundreds of teachers annually risk serious vocal abuse, serious vocal fold RSI.

Voice Care Provision

While education authorities give vocal training a low priority so too does the teaching profession. Perhaps more teachers should have cited vocal fold RSI and looked for compensation when having to leave the profession because their voices could no longer meet the demands of their professional role. Alongside this wastage to the profession should be set the many hundreds of hours lost through laryngitis, episodic voice loss and vocal abuse. If we look at the numbers of teachers who present with voice problems in speech and language therapy clinics we find they are extensive. Teachers form a large proportion of their voice case load. In 1992, figures were collected from forty clinics throughout the United Kingdom for the month of June. This recorded that 122 teachers were currently in treatment for voice disorders, forty-seven teachers were new referrals and ninety-three teachers were on review. This gave an average figure of 6.7 teachers per clinic. This figure however only accounts for those teachers who sought help; many teachers never get as far as the speech and language therapy clinic. For many teachers to admit that they have a problem, which potentially may affect their ability to teach, would make them feel too vulnerable. This is particularly true when one looks at the demographic changes in the United Kingdom which have shown a reduction in the school-age population over successive years. Fewer children being born has had an adverse effect on teacher numbers with proportionately fewer teachers being needed, fewer posts being available and therefore a greater pressure on those in work to retain their jobs. In this climate teachers who are vocally vulnerable are not likely to advertise the fact by admitting to voice problems, even if there is likely to be a sympathetic response from their head teacher. Teachers who have had voice problems, when questioned, reported that when this had been brought to the attention of the school there had been support from the relevant authorities (Martin 1994). There is however much anecdotal evidence to suggest that many teachers arrange therapy sessions out of school hours and some never mention the fact that they are undergoing therapy to colleagues or pupils. For those teachers who do not seek help their only recourse is to try and continue to teach through periods of laryngitis or voice loss...until the next time. For teachers in the USA the huge cost of health care is often a factor in a teacher's ability to have therapy. If their health insurance does not cover the cost of speech and language therapy then teachers are unable to get help. American teachers have reported to us that because the high cost of insurance was too much for them to sustain, they were effectively unable to do anything other than resign from the profession.

In the United Kingdom organisations like The British Voice Association, the British Association for Performing Arts Medicine, the Voice Care Network and many concerned interdisciplinary voice clinics offer treatment from a laryngologist, speech and language therapist and sometimes an osteopath or Alexander teacher and are attempting to address the needs of teachers by offering preventative training courses and workshops. In Sweden, the University of Gothenburg began a voice course for their employees in 1992 where university teachers were given weekly voice training in small groups. It appears that increasingly the needs of the teaching profession are being addressed but regrettably still only in limited ways.

Many teachers do effect temporary improvement through voice rest, while a significant number of teachers simply 'put up with it'. It is unfortunate that for most people, and here we are looking in general terms at the population at large, incidents of voice loss or vocal abuse remain a very low priority on the scale of significant illness – indeed there still exists what might be described as a rather *laissez faire* attitude to voice problems. The perception is that vocal dysfunction is something to be treated as an occasional 'hazard', rather than attributing it appropriately to the effects of vocal abuse and misuse. Unfortunately this attitude leads to a spiral of periodic voice loss, followed by periods of remission due to vocal rest and a gradual acceptance that perhaps the voice is not as good as it was, but it will probably never be any better. Slowly there is a loss of ability to critically appraise the voice and to notice changes. Often a voice can become deeper over a period of time without the teacher or individual (it is not only teachers who are rather negligent with their voices) ever being aware of it. It is only on a clinical assessment that questions arise as to whether a particular pitch or level is really appropriate for the individual. If proper voice training was given as part of teacher training most teachers would then be able to monitor and sustain their own voice effectively throughout their working life. For a small number of vocally vulnerable teachers, problems might still occur but it would be a much reduced number in comparison to the current situation. In addition it would be a much more cost-effective solution to a problem which currently costs education authorities huge sums in lost time and teacher replacements.

Chapter 2
The Effects of Teaching on the Voice

In the teachers' workshops we ran in London and the South East of England in conjunction with the Voice Care and Development for Teachers Project, we encountered numerous teachers who said they had been looking for many years for some sort of support group for their vocal problems. They were under the mistaken impression that they were the only ones suffering from vocal difficulties. They remarked that while other teachers seemed to suffer voice loss, this was attributed to colds or a virus and no connection between voice use and voice loss was made. Many teachers came back to a second in-service training day because they needed and wanted to retain contact with a group in order to reassure themselves that they had a legitimate problem and that there was a solution. It was through these individuals that we were able to glean much of our understanding of the complexity of the problems facing the teacher. Women far outnumbered men at these workshops and it is generally the case that men suffer fewer episodes of voice loss than women, due to their greater ability to produce volume without strain and the greater resonance and therefore carrying power of the male voice. There are, of course, exceptions to every rule and those men who attended the workshops were sometimes very anxious about their voices and frequently under stress. They often felt their problem was due to some shortcoming within themselves and were relieved to know they were not alone, but that they were suffering from a common occupational condition, which could in the long term be remedied and prevented from recurring.

What Type of Training?

The type of voice training required by the teacher is not unlike that required by the actor. The voice is a physical instrument and therefore training must be given in posture and alignment, efficient use of effort, breathing, voice production, projection and safe shouting, interpretative skills and vocal health. The teachers we have worked with have been in agreement in what they perceived to be the effects of teaching on the voice. These tended to be negative perceptions and it was usually felt that the voice could not operate efficiently over a sustained period of time, for most people a full working day was felt to be too long. This should not be the case; the voice, when used efficiently and therefore effectively, can 'work' for as long as necessary without presenting problems, so long as the environmental conditions are reasonable and the voice remains healthy.

Interestingly no one said that their voice had strengthened with use or that they had developed the ability to read effectively for longer periods of time, whereas actors who have had voice training often remark that their voice strengthens over the duration of the run of a play, generally building in resonance, flexibility and range.

Most of the teachers we spoke to were those already encountering problems, but even those who said they did not have a problem reported vocal tiredness. This is not a specific or easily definable feeling and so is fairly unreliable to document. What we are reporting are the subjective opinions of teachers describing their own voices. The words and phrases used to answer the question, 'What are the effects of teaching on your voice?' were: 'tiredness', 'hoarseness', 'dryness', 'a lack of power', 'an inability to communicate effectively', 'a lack of flexibility', 'a tight and constricted feeling', 'soreness', 'a rasping quality', 'monotony', 'my voice fading after a few hours' and 'feeling that you are stuck on one note'. Many of these descriptions herald a need for help and fall into the category of early warning signals.

Early Warning Signals

All voice users should be aware of the following early warning signals and should seek referral if any one or a number occur:

- Recurring loss of voice
- Diminution in range and flexibility
- Pain or discomfort in the area of the larynx
- A marked change in the pitch of the voice following an incident of vocal misuse
- A voice that does not return to normal after a cold or a bout of laryngitis

- A loss of volume with accompanying increase in effort to achieve previous loudness
- A feeling of having a 'lump in the throat'
- Any loss of hearing

Medical Referral

Most of us are notoriously bad at identifying specific muscles or ligaments and so a voice problem which may arise from muscular tension is often interpreted as a sore throat. Teachers reported that they had been to their doctor to seek help and, possibly because they were unable to clearly describe their voice problem, had left the surgery without the advice and help they sought, but clutching a prescription for antibiotics. Few doctors sent teachers to a laryngologist or suggested that there might be a postural solution to the problem or that working on breath and voice production might provide the solution. Few doctors asked the appropriate questions.

The doctor should ask:

- How long has the problem existed?
- Is it related to a cold or flu?
- Does the individual suffer from any allergies?
- Has anything precipitated the voice problem, such as shouting?
- Does it follow a pattern, does it occur at the same time each term?
- Is the atmosphere in the classroom dry?
- What is the water intake of the individual?
- How does the individual use their body in relation to the height of the desks and the blackboard?
- Could individual teaching style be a contributing factor?
- Does the individual suffer from backache, neckache, or other physical problems?
- Does the individual get a feeling of a lump in the throat?
- Does the individual suffer from professional or personal stress?

Within the United Kingdom there are presently considerable demands on doctors and consequent limits on their consultation times, so it is possible that voice problems are not always given the attention they deserve. On occasions teachers complain that the doctor's initial response is often to write out a prescription. This action however often magnifies the problem for the teacher whose immediate reaction is to think, 'I'm making a fuss about nothing' or 'It's no wonder my voice is sore, I'm obviously not a good teacher' or 'This is what happens to teachers' voices'. Consequently many individuals do not return to the doctor believing they just have to 'live with it'. Many of the teachers who came on our courses said they really had believed that it was not a bad enough problem to 'moan about' in the staffroom or to take time off for. One teacher said, 'It's not like an ankle, when you sprain your ankle everyone can see you are in trouble and they sympathise: no one can see the voice so they often ignore it'. Another teacher said, 'When my voice is bad, people occasionally say "you've got a nasty cold". I don't bother to explain I don't have a cold at all.' Another remark we heard frequently was, 'Well you can't really take time off for a bad voice, not like you could for tonsillitis, you don't *feel* ill when your voice is bad.'

Describing the Symptom

Tiredness

The terminology for voice problems is very subjective, but there are a number of frequently used terms, notably, 'I get hoarse' or 'My voice feels tired.' When enquiring further into the 'feelings' of tiredness we heard comments like: 'My voice gets dry and sore', 'I keep having to swallow', 'It's like there is a tight band around my throat', 'It fades away in the middle of the sentence', 'I have no power', 'I can start off on a reasonable pitch but as I go on it gets higher and higher.'

The reported 'tiredness' is usually caused by ineffective production of the voice. The muscles used to produce sound are used in other functions, such as lifting, pushing, giving birth, coughing and keeping foreign bodies from getting into the lungs. As they have this innate muscularity, they are also capable of being inadvertently over-used in the production of the voice. When used efficiently, the voice does not tire. When used without proper breath support, with poorly aligned body posture and when more muscles than those necessary for the purpose are used, the voice begins to tire.

Hoarseness

Hoarseness usually refers to the reedy, often husky vocal quality caused by the vocal folds only being partly vibrated, because they are swollen. It is not necessarily accompanied by any pain or discomfort, although it may be. The voice in this condition is sometimes described as attractive or even 'sexy' and because of this sufferers often enjoy the compliments instead of resting the voice in order to reduce swelling and allow the vocal folds to return to their natural state.

Another possible reason for the hoarse sound is dehydration caused by insufficient water intake. The voice needs to be lubricated at all times and classrooms can be artificially dry and overheated. Teachers are often discouraged from drinking during class but this is not a sensible rule. The more an individual has to speak, the more they should drink. The best liquid is water, as tea and coffee have dehydrating properties and alcohol is particularly drying. Many people when asked whether they drink enough will respond that they do, only to discover that they are drinking the wrong kind of liquids.

Similar symptoms may be experienced with laryngitis: in extreme cases the voice may vanish altogether or diminish to a whisper. Teachers are generally dedicated to their work and tend to 'soldier on', ignoring the problem. Ignoring the problem is not to be encouraged because when the vocal folds are swollen and the closure is incomplete, the muscles of the larynx have to overwork in order to produce a sound. The volume required to reach the back of the classroom or, worse still, to control a group of noisy children on the sports field, results in real strain and can in severe cases damage the folds.

It is possible that an allergic reaction may be responsible for the hoarse quality. This can be related to hayfever or pollution allergies and can result in either a reduction in the lubrication of the vocal folds, or an abundance of mucous. Asthma with its consequential effect of reducing lung capacity can contribute to vocal strain and hoarseness. It is often a misplaced stoicism that encourages the teacher to continue under these conditions: the voice in this state is seldom effective. The husky voice can have the effect of making an audience feel tired and inattentive. The emotional edge to the voice has gone and the tension that goes into producing the sound becomes the quality that is listened to. It is interesting to observe an audience being addressed by a 'hoarse' speaker, they often clear their throats in sympathy or even cough.

What causes hoarseness?

If there is no cold or infection there is probably a functional reason for the hoarse sound of the voice. It could be that the individual's posture is not conducive to easy efficient production of the voice, so that the muscles overwork, resulting in 'strain'. In an otherwise healthy voice, there is usually a fairly easily correctable reason for the problem, which is very often linked to breathing. A fuller description of breathing will be given in Chapter 4 but it is important to say here that the breath is responsible for the vibration of the folds and if that breath is either not powerful enough to set the folds in motion, or is not synchronised with the activity of voice, problems can occur. Breath is closely linked to the emotional life of us all and so when we are under stress we are more likely to 'block' or inhibit the very natural and normal activity of breathing.

The Teacher's Perspective

We were very fortunate in gaining the support of the staff at a primary school in south east London who helped us to conduct a small-scale survey. This survey allowed us to explore some of the problems the teachers encountered in terms of how their own voices 'performed' under teaching conditions and how confident or otherwise they felt with their own level of language use. The school is in a residential area with no major discipline problems and the children are aged from rising five to eleven years old. There is a hearing unit attached to the school which means that hearing impaired children are integrated into the school. There are some children with other special needs within the school but these represent a small percentage of the school population.

Of those staff who completed the questionnaire 78% had no work on their voice during their training, 87% said that their voice had failed at some point in their professional life, becoming croaky, hoarse, or husky, and 21% of those questioned said their voice had disappeared altogether. When asked, 'Does your throat ever get tight?' 87% said yes and 65% said they thought this was a common complaint. Despite the difficulties they experienced with their voices, 88% said that it conveyed the qualities that they wanted to convey, but when asked to describe their voice some of the adjectives used were, 'squeaky', 'quite weak', 'loud', 'husky', 'creaky', 'low pitched'. Only 22% were happy with their voice as it was. When asked to name the most difficult vocal situation that they encountered, 'parents' evenings' were named by 34% of the teachers, with 23% citing 'reprimanding the class' as the most difficult vocal situation.

The teachers were asked if they saw themselves as performers and all those questioned said 'yes'. When asked how confident they were with spoken language, 65% said they were confident, but when asked if their confidence would be the same with a different age group, only 22% said 'yes'.

When asked what aspects of teaching they were not fully prepared for in college, their answers ranged from drama and story-telling, the pastoral role of a teacher, the stamina required, the work levels, to the amount of talking, the use of the voice and behaviour management skills.

This survey only looked at one primary school but we think that it is safe to suggest that these results would be replicated in almost every school in the British Isles and undoubtedly there are similar problems worldwide. Could it be said that voice problems within the teaching profession have reached epidemic proportions?

To look at the human face of these statistics we offer three case histories.

Case Study: Avril

An example of the impact that the demands of teaching make on the voice is seen in the case of Avril. Avril is 38 years old, a mother of three who is married to a man whose job involves her in a considerable amount of entertaining and socialising. Avril is therefore accustomed to using her voice in a social setting and often amongst large noisy groups. Deciding to retrain as a teacher Avril enrolled on a Post Graduate Certificate in Education course. Before her marriage she had trained as a specialist teacher of Speech and Drama and had also worked as a professional actress in a touring educational theatre group. This work had been both tiring and demanding vocally but she had her training and technique to draw upon. The company often performed twice and sometimes three times a day and travelled great distances between schools. As the plays were participatory she was involved in controlling the often very large groups but never experienced any vocal problems. After her period with the Theatre in Education group she performed in musicals and rock operas, again never experiencing vocal difficulties. A period of fifteen years elapsed, during which she left the theatre and worked as a personal assistant in broadcasting and had her three children. She stopped working on her voice during this time but kept herself physically fit by working out in a gymnasium and doing aerobic exercises.

Once she found herself in the classroom she was amazed and rather shocked to find that at the end of the day her voice felt tired and sore. 'I felt as if I would develop nodules if I didn't do something about it,' she said. 'I realised I must go back to working on my breathing because I never had these problems when I acted'. Asked why she thought this was so, she replied, 'When you are acting you are very aware of technique. Breath support is part of the job and is integrated into the performance. My teaching practice took place in a school where discipline was a problem. I found myself constantly having to reprimand the children. My actions were spontaneous and I suppose I felt out of control at times. I had lost my objectivity and my reactions were subjective.'

With someone who has previously experienced the ability to support the voice, it is easy to remind them of the sensations and to help them to re-establish healthy usage. As Avril had kept fit and in touch with her body her breathing muscles did not take long to re-establish their previous tone. Avril recognised the effect on her voice of stress, which in her case was related to the additional work and organisation involved in doing first her BA degree and then the PGCE. As so often happens with a mature student, she had taken her studies extremely seriously and achieved excellent grades. In addition, however, she had had to juggle her children's needs, both practical and emotional, with the social demands of her husband's career, running the home and finding time to study.

Case Study: Theresa

Another interesting case is that of Theresa. We met her when she became aware of her need to address her vocal problem. She had a history of recurring voice loss and sounded husky even when her voice was at it best She is not a smoker but described her voice as sounding like that of a heavy smoker. She noticed that her voice was at its worst after a night in the pub, after singing or after talking for sustained periods.

The most impressive and appealing quality about Theresa is her natural exuberance, she is enormously positive and personable and is constantly 'on the go'; her energy seems boundless. As a single mother she has to cope with stress, and her coping strategy is to meet life's challenges 'head on', but her personal strength is also the reason her tensions are manifested in her voice. Her energy emanates from the neck and shoulder area and while she is able to relax given time, she does not do so easily. Her breath is shallow and she tends to hold onto it, rather than to release it into voice and speech. Her habitual head/neck alignment is to position her head in front of her shoulders, leading to considerable strain on the muscles of the neck and shoulders and therefore the laryngeal structure is under stress. She speaks loudly and rapidly, complains of dryness and a feeling of tightness in the larynx. Her general effort level is high.

Theresa is an excellent example of the important relationship between physicality and the voice. There is nothing wrong with her voice but the stresses and strains that non-alignment of the spine, shoulders, neck and head have placed upon her larynx, plus the overwork she forces upon her laryngeal muscles, have produced a set of circumstances which she perceives as a 'voice' problem. Add to this the poor use of breath and the emotional stresses involved with being a single working mother and the result is that her voice is 'under attack'.

To counter these problems, Theresa has enormous resources. She has the intelligence to perceive that all is not well and has the will and ability to do something about it. She is a pliable individual open to change. She has had counselling from a qualified therapist over the break-up of her relationship with her child's father and has a great deal of self-knowledge and motivation. The enthusiasm that produced the problem is the best weapon she has to deal with it.

Case Study: Hazel

Hazel is an art student whom we met while she was working as a dresser at one of the London theatres. Hazel had been a teacher for ten years but had been forced to give up work because she developed vocal nodules. The progression from a healthy voice at the beginning of her career to a voice unable to cope with the demands of the profession was a fairly lengthy process. Vocal nodules begin as soft small red swellings on the edges of the vocal folds, but in time without treatment they will harden, become fibrous and white in colour. With early treatment and attention to good vocal hygiene and usage they will disappear, but if left untreated they often require surgical removal, as in Hazel's case.

Two issues which she highlighted as contributing factors were that she was working as a primary school teacher with seven-year-old Bangladeshi children in an open plan school. The children were naturally very vocal and as a teacher she admits that she encouraged quite a noisy working environment, partly because there was a need for the children to speak in order to progress in English, so the more talking that went on the better, and also, as the children were naturally noisy, she liked to encourage them to be noisy and she enjoyed a noisy, busy environment. The open plan class arrangement meant that there were noises from the other classes, so in order to be heard Hazel had to raise her voice over the ambient noise in addition to the noise of the thirty children she was teaching. The general noise level was high as there were no partitions between classes, just pillars to define the space.

In addition to her teaching load Hazel used to work with puppets for which she had not had any formal training. The effect on her voice from postural factors was considerable as she moved from standing to crouching positions and of course she often spoke with her head tipped back. As well as this less than ideal position for voicing, she also told us that she spoke regularly to children at a distance, raising her voice to do so. As Hazel said, 'You are encouraged to talk all the time from 9am to 3:30pm, using a raised pitch for nearly all this time.' Hazel took water into the classroom, but generally water in the classroom was not encouraged and there was no water near the radiator or any attempt to humidify the room. Hazel reported there had been no help or advice towards looking after her voice or any suggestion that she should be aware of it when she was training. At college she was simply told, 'Your voice is your control' so there were no strategies on offer to help students; indeed she said that it was, 'all a question of luck'.

In Hazel's case there was no evidence of vocal vulnerability either as a student or teacher. She had enjoyed working in the noisy, lively environment of the school which she admitted was quite stressful but very friendly, and it had taken her a long time to realise there was a real problem with her voice which initially became husky. She subsequently realised that she needed to use a lot of effort to talk and could not get volume. For a while she lost her voice completely.

Realising that there was a problem she went to her doctor who fortunately took it seriously and referred her to a specialist straight away. Hazel was lucky in that the school was most supportive and she was able to have an appointment time at 4 pm which meant that she only missed the last half hour of school. Hazel said the problem that many teachers experience is the feeling of guilt when taking time off. There was no budget at her school to cover supply teaching, so if she took a day off funds for a supply teacher were used which could otherwise have gone to replace equipment or buy some item that was much needed. Teachers at her school made every effort to go into school unless desperately ill. Equally she reported that there was already so much time taken out of the school week by paper work, testing of children and meetings, that there was a great desire on the part of all staff to minimise the time spent away.

Hazel was fortunate in that she was able to go on to art college and retrain, as otherwise her voice problems would have meant that she would have had to take six months off. Hazel agreed that she had always taken her voice for granted, never bothered about it and in her words 'produced it haphazardly'. The year that her voice became a problem was the first year of the National Curriculum which increased her workload dramatically. Another contributory factor she felt was that 95% of the school population was Asian in an area which was adjacent to a district which had elected members of the British National Front to the district council. This created considerable stress within the area, although Hazel said that there were no discipline problems at her school. Hazel agreed that this extreme external social stress was possibly a contributory factor, as environmental factors are closely linked to vocal abuse and misuse.

In looking at factors such as diet, Hazel said she used to eat very spicy food but did not eat late at night and did not drink, although she regularly smoked ten cigarettes a day and had done so from the age of fifteen. She stopped smoking when her voice problems were identified.

On a personal level Hazel found that her loss of voice was very distressing, not only was it quite painful to talk but it was amazingly debilitating. As a teacher she had become used to 'arranging' things with her voice, which she likened to conducting. She had 'conducted' with her voice and felt completely helpless and feeble without it. Her voice had been like a tool, one that she suddenly could not use. At the end of each day she was really tired and felt quite ill: she found it difficult to breathe and the strain of speaking all the time was very taxing. It seemed to her as though she was talking at the top of her voice, yet only a little sound was emerging and quite often she could not speak at all. Hazel had voice therapy for almost a year. During this time she could not talk at night and as a result she stopped going out. She said that she felt very isolated as there is great pressure to speak in company and when she could not do so comfortably, she got quite depressed.

Her experience of voice loss was one of isolation and distress with accompanying periods of depression. Eventually Hazel's voice returned but she had to leave the profession as her voice would not have supported the demands of a teaching career. Even now Hazel still has periods of vocal strain if she talks in clubs and pubs over noise, so she remains vigilant about avoiding situations which may be vocally taxing. She will 'warm up' now if she is going to have to talk for any length of time, and drinks a lot of water, drinking herbal teas in preference to coffee or tea, and she uses steam if she has been misusing her voice. Hazel commented that when she lost her voice she felt as though she was 'shut into a box' and couldn't communicate. She was aware of being treated differently in shops, and social occasions were an enormous pressure when she could not talk. The invisibility of her injury was difficult, as was the uncertainty of achieving voice, as there was no certainty before she spoke that she would be able to produce sound. In addition she reported that when she lost her voice initially she didn't know if it would ever come back, which made her incredibly anxious.

Hazel's experience is one that must be familiar to many readers and is perhaps a useful illustration of the effects of teaching on one teacher's voice. This exciting and imaginative teacher is now lost to the profession. More specific help during her three-year training course could have avoided the problems she encountered.

Chapter 3
The Effect on the Voice of External Stress Factors

Several years ago there was a period of bitter unrest within the teaching profession in the United Kingdom. Teachers objected to the increased demands that the introduction of the National Curriculum imposed and indeed there was a general feeling of militancy among teachers which emanated in part from a feeling within the profession that there was little public recognition of the work that teachers undertook and even less regard for teachers as professionals working in a very stressful environment. There was and is a general misperception that the teacher has short working days and long holidays, so when issues relating to salary and working practices were raised the public had very little sympathy for some of the teachers' legitimate complaints.

One of the difficulties within the profession currently is that there has been a general erosion of teachers' salary scales in terms of a national average, so that currently in the United Kingdom teacher and lecturer salary scales fall well below those within the commercial and industrial sectors. A more worrying trend, highlighted by the Audit Commission in the United Kingdom in 1994, was that local management of schools has led some head teachers and governors to appoint less experienced teachers because they are cheaper to employ. Teachers' unions reported that as schools seek to save money, more experienced and expensive teachers were being forced out of jobs. This of course has a critical effect on the balance of experience within schools, it has implications for younger teachers who will find that the 'mentoring' aspect which, as a newly qualified teacher they would expect to find, is not available. In addition it profoundly affects teacher morale with the implication that experience counts for little and financial considerations are a major criterion in teacher selection. Increasingly teachers find themselves in the unhappy position of not being able to recommend the profession to students who want to make teaching a career.

Some of the antipathy to the teachers' concerns might have been due in part to a lack of ability by those 'fighting' for the teachers to communicate their demands in a way that would win over the general public and not alienate them. Recent linguistic studies have clearly illustrated the national differences that exist in communication styles, many cultures for example see arguing as a pleasurable sign of intimacy as well as a game. Deborah Tannen (1991) suggests that viewing a friendly conversation in Greece is, for Americans, like viewing an argument and indeed it appears even more heated than an argument would do in America. Linguist Deborah Schiffrin (1984) showed that in the conversations of working class Jewish Eastern European speakers in Philadelphia, friendly argument was a means of being sociable. The difficulty is that for many British people, overt displays of emotion either vocal, linguistic or indeed physical are considered alien, while to some individuals they demonstrate a lack of control. The fervour with which the teachers' leaders took up their cause may have unwittingly contributed to the lack of widespread public support, particularly when appearing on television where even the most moderate gesture can appear extreme.

The Effect of Work Factors

Teachers in the United Kingdom report that they are currently overwhelmed with work, in large part by the amount of paper work that is generated by the demands of the National Curriculum and in addition by the need to take on greater and greater responsibility after very little time in teaching. Posts of special responsibility, after-school activities, league sports teams, music or drama events and the integration of special needs children within mainstream schooling, all create additional pressures for the teacher. As a result teachers are, in increasing numbers, bowing out of teaching, the number of teachers ending their careers early because of ill health has trebled in the UK since the early 1980s and now only one teacher in five works on to the statutory retirement age, according to figures published by the National Association of Head Teachers in 1994. As the population's overall health had improved over the previous 12 years the high incidence of medical retirements reflected, in the Association's opinion, the prevalence of stress-related illness.

Levels of Stress

There are a significant number of incidents which reach the British national press involving teachers, such as sexual harassment of teachers by pupils, problems of discipline, the inability of teachers to instil and maintain discipline and the understandable unease within the profession when faced with a growing number of pupils who are physically violent towards them.

The education system in the United Kingdom has been subject to a myriad of changes; changes in the requirements of the National Curriculum, changes in the status of schools; schools that can opt out, schools that have to stay in, schools that were known as schools and are now city technology centres, schools that were independent and one sex that are now co-educational, schools that cannot achieve the necessary pupil numbers and schools that attempt to continue to function, burdened by underfunding and consequent overburdening of teachers. In many areas of education staff feel devalued and unable to function effectively.

The Link between Stress and the Voice

The relationship between voice, emotion and physical state has been clearly established for many years by those working with voice, although this information is possibly less well disseminated to the public at large. Many within the teaching profession are unaware of the links between voice and emotion and the effect of physical and mental stress on the voice.

The link between self-esteem, ego and voice is more clearly understood if the physical changes that occur in a state of low esteem are considered. Possibly the most noticeable changes are postural, such as lowered eye levels, when the individual rarely looks straight ahead but tends to keep their eyes looking downwards towards the floor. Allied to this lowered eye level are slumped shoulders, rounded back and a much more contained, introverted posture, with accumulated tension in the shoulders, neck and jaw. Physiological changes due to stress-related factors such as shallow breathing patterns, a faster breath rate, and changes in the chemical balance within the body all occur. These cumulative changes will often have the effect of making the individual feel completely exhausted and unable to function effectively.

In Chapter 4 we look at the structure of the larynx and explain in simple but clear terms how voice is produced. In order for voicing to occur easily and effortlessly, all the various components, both mental and mechanical, that make up the vocal process need to function at optimum efficiency and be free from tension. The links between the various components will be looked at in detail, but it is worthwhile emphasising here that voice, mood and emotion are very closely linked. When a high level of stress is added to the less than ideal circumstances in which teachers use their voices, we can clearly see why teachers often experience voice problems.

While considering the effects of stress on the voice and the current high levels of stress within the teaching profession, it is also worth considering the high proportion of women versus men in the profession. It would be invidious to suggest that women are more likely than men to suffer professionally from stress, but many women return to teaching after they have children, yet the fact that the school time table represents only a small proportion of the teaching 'day' which extends to after-school activities, preparation and marking, is often not recognised and women teachers may find that their family role sits uneasily with their professional role. This dual role is clearly implicated in the cycle of stress which is so much part of the teacher's life and which many see as a predisposing factor in their voice problems. An additional factor is the physiological difference between the male and female larynx and the endocrinological changes that occur which may on occasion make women more vocally 'at risk' than their male colleagues.

The Effects of Stress

The voice is a very precise stress indicator. A rather obvious but appropriate example is the way in which people's moods may be judged on the telephone, where we have no indicator other than the voice; we cannot see facial expression, body posture or gestures and all we have is a voice saying 'hello'. We must all have experience of being both the caller and the called, when we have accurately identified the other person's mood and when someone has identified our mood by our initial greeting. We 'are' our voice; our energy levels, our mood, our physical health are all reflected in our voice.

When we are tired the muscular processes of voicing will be less flexible. The expression 'I was so tired I could hardly say a word' is one that is very familiar and which must, at one time or another, have been experienced by us all. While it tends to be thought of as referring to the physical process of actually articulating what we are thinking, it should also be remembered that speech is a highly complicated process, not only a physical but also an emotional and mental process. The mental processes involved in 'saying a word' are being studied and defined and are not yet completely understood.

Evidence of the complicated structures required to speak is most vividly seen when there is a breakdown in the processes, for example when people have a stroke or suffer from some degenerative nervous condition, like Parkinson's Disease or Muscular Dystrophy. In a less dramatic way we can probably all reflect on situations where we just couldn't remember the word that we wanted – we can think of another word, but we know that it is not the specific word for which we are searching. Then there is the situation where helpful listeners supply a variety of words which they think are appropriate, but they are not the one that we are trying to vocalise. This is slightly different from the 'It's on the tip of my tongue' syndrome. Whereas the 'tip of the tongue' syndrome can occur at any time, the forgetting of perfectly simple words or losing the train of thought are often aggravated by tiredness and in some instances tension and stress.

Simply forgetting a word or not being able to use the right word would appear to be rather a minor problem but, on the contrary, for those to whom it happens with regularity it is a very real problem. We can think of stammerers who report that the constant 'helpful' supplying of words when they block is incredibly irritating. Indeed on a personal level, one of the authors, having spent several years living in a European country, reported that while she could cope perfectly well in the language, her lack of a more complete vocabulary meant that on occasions she was unable to find a literal translation for what she wanted to say and had to substitute a word that roughly expressed the same sense but was not exactly right.

Coping with Change

In the author's experience this inability to find the right word changed the way in which she felt about herself; she wasn't reflecting her feelings adequately and this she found very disconcerting. Teachers whose first language is not English can experience this in terms of the rhythm of their speech, indeed where one language is used at home and another in the teaching environment, similar problems may occur. Sometimes teachers experience this same sense of dislocation not because of a change in language but because the framework within which they teach changes. Syllabus changes will mean that teachers have to suddenly learn new material and often feel uncomfortable with the short period of time they are given to assimilate it. How many teachers who are qualified to teach one subject suddenly find themselves having to teach another with which they are comparatively unfamiliar, having to keep one step ahead of the class? This is not to suggest that teachers want to collude in apparently offering less than expert tuition, but simply that limits imposed by the pupil/staff ratio and the subject choices made by pupils mean that this does occur. The level of tension that is engendered is considerable, the majority of teachers want to be prepared, to be confident about the subject and to feel that they can legitimately be 'the expert'. The difficulty for teachers lies in trying to reconcile the demands of the school administration and their own needs, and on most occasions the requirements of the school take precedence. One newly qualified but mature teacher told us that she feared that at the end of her first year of teaching she would be required by the head teacher to take on a post of special responsibility which she felt quite unable to do. She followed this by saying: 'I just don't feel I have the skills or the experience to be able to cope.'

If one assumes that this is not an isolated case, then there must be many teachers struggling to maintain their position against overwhelming administrative and professional demands. In addition to these professional demands teachers are not immune to the effects of stress within their personal lives, for example bereavement, miscarriage, divorce, redundancy of a partner and prolonged chronic illness, which do not prevent them from teaching but do have a very debilitating effect.

One teacher we spoke to had had a chronic upper respiratory tract infection for eight months. She was a music teacher who as a result of this upper respiratory tract infection had experienced voice and intermittent hearing problems, which resulted in her not being able to vocally control her class, and in addition she noticed that her singing range had diminished by half. This teacher had not been referred to a voice specialist and simple strategies of voice care and conservation had never been suggested. In addition to voice problems relating to illness, teachers also frequently report voice problems related to classroom discipline or indeed to incidents with individual pupils. Teachers who have been teaching for years and have been completely free from voice problems may suddenly experience voice problems which they can directly relate to difficulty with a particular pupil. Their perception is that as they became more stressed by the situation so they experienced voice problems.

While for some the stress that results from these sorts of situations may be controlled, for others the same level of stress can result in a vocal problem, sleeplessness, depression or anxiety attacks. One result of this is physiological; when we are under prolonged periods of stress, large amounts of adrenalin and noradrenalin are produced which have a cumulative physiological effect. The release of these chemicals means that the individual will be able to maintain their activities for a period of time, indeed even get that extra 'buzz' that people experience when working at full stretch, but the cumulative effect is that these unusually high levels of noradrenalin in the body will contribute to a sudden feeling of complete exhaustion unrelated to physical effort, when the individual feels unable to do anything apart from lying down and sleeping. Some teachers experience this effect at the end of every term, for other people this is an occasional episode triggered when the cumulative effects of personal and professional stresses become too much.

Changes in Vocal Quality

This physiological change has its effect on the voice, and the tired and strained vocal quality with which teachers present at the end of term is a well-known phenomena in staffrooms all over the world. Equally, teachers will report that as well as having voice problems at the end of term many experience problems at the beginning of term when returning after a long summer break. One of the reasons for this is that during the summer holiday period the teacher has been able to effect some form of 'damage limitation' as far as their voice is concerned. Periods of speaking with less effort and in a more vocally friendly environment allow the voice to return to a more natural setting. Once the teacher returns to the school environment there is an increase in stress and tension levels which means that the voice has to re-adjust to a different setting and once the 'new' setting is established, the voice becomes clearer. Our individual response to stress and tension cannot be absolutely anticipated; we can predict danger areas but we do not know definitely what the effects will be. Again some teachers can demonstrate amazing vocal resilience for years only to find that completely without warning their voice disappears without any apparent overloading, while other teachers will experience mild vocal symptoms for years and these will never get any worse nor become unmanageable. What we do know however is that most teachers and indeed most voice patients will report the same feelings; diminution of vocal flexibility, range, loudness, or ease of voicing, leads to an erosion of their concept of self. The inability to properly express feelings, emotions and thoughts because of voice loss due to vocal abuse or misuse is very alienating.

Environmental Factors

How can teachers better anticipate factors which will increase the likelihood of vocal strain? We have discussed the potential stress triggers and identified emotional and physical factors that can affect voice quality. Looking at environmental factors we need to take into account issues like overcrowding and lack of space within the school. Well-documented evidence (notably studies by the psychologist Skinner with the rat population) show that where individuals have to live and work in overcrowded conditions the levels of tension rise and this increase is reflected in heightened feelings of aggression and violence. For many teachers the issues of overcrowding are considered only in terms of class size. Increases in class size are cited as giving teachers problems related to actual teaching efficiency. How can you teach forty children in one class? How can you respond to the needs of every child? How can you keep control? There is also the issue of overcrowding and psychological response. It is clear that if one adds feelings of tension arising from overcrowding to the difficulty of controlling large numbers of children the resulting cocktail is fairly potent. Teachers deserve to have some professional advice in terms of the new developments in ergonomics and to try and limit problems of overcrowding if at all possible. Apart from the central issue of too many people in too small a space it is also important to look at the effect it has on the pupils who are equally influenced by the space in which they work. Fortunately the children do have the twice daily option of racing madly around a playground shouting and screaming, so releasing tension in a physical way. Indeed sports lessons offer a similar release from tension but regrettably the Secretary of State for Education has not yet seen fit to introduce the Japanese style of managing stress by stipulating that a punch bag is provided in every staffroom and an acoustically sealed rest room is available to staff as an alternative to a padded cell!

Physiological Effects of Stress

Stress of course affects everyone, it is a necessary and essential part of our lives and is the result of interaction between us and our environment. Stress is to some extent an adaptive response by the body to changes in the environment. For example if we were confronted by a man-eating lion we would need to activate our stress response in order to be ready to stand and fight or turn and run. Today it is less likely that we will be confronted by any man-eating predators, but instead we have to deal with an urban jungle or, as teachers sometimes describe their place of work, a 'blackboard jungle', and for many individuals the threat of physical, emotional and psychological pain is ever present, if not actually encountered. We live in a world where the changes we face have dramatically increased and although we may not meet the lion, we respond to situations as though the lion was there. We activate the stress response but as we cannot activate the accompanying physical response, we become impatient, angry and irritated instead.

Competitiveness in the job market and in society in general is endemic. Teachers often find themselves being pulled along by emotional and social demands as well as the demands of their job. Whether it is warranted or not, our stress response is activated, but as we cannot leap into action by hitting out or engaging in physical conflict we keep these feelings suppressed and hit out in other ways, either verbally or through drugs, alcohol or nicotine addiction. In the present climate teachers are also limited in their relationships with students because of the contradictions implicit in the teacher/pupil relationship. The teacher is expected to discipline the child, comfort the child and form a relationship with the child without contravening the codes of conduct. For many teachers the real fear of their actions being misconstrued as abuse is a limiting and stressful factor in their professional practice.

Many doctors now recognise that it is in the inhibition of the physical response to stress that the danger to our health lies. Our body defences are in a constant state of activation and this can lead to ill health. The irony is that the stress response which is supposed to save us from the perils of the man-eating lion does in some cases contribute to our death. So what happens at a physiological level when we are confronted by an actual life-threatening situation, when we move into 'fight or flight' mode?

Information about our environment is picked up by our senses which is then passed to our brain for processing. If the situation is potentially dangerous we activate the stress response and make a decision as to whether we can best meet the demand by staying and fighting or turning and fleeing, and both of these actions will require different physiological responses. If, however, the situation is one with which we can cope, the stress response will remain within the normal zone.

Once the brain has processed the information and decided on an appropriate response, instructions in the form of small electrical impulses are sent along nerves to the body parts and the required action occurs. In the case of a decision to stay and fight or when one needs a sustained effort to gain control over a situation, the brain activates the production of noradrenalin to prepare the body for a fight. If the decision is made to run and flee the production of increased amounts of adrenalin is signalled, which increases the heart rate and imbues the individual with plenty of energy for the muscular activity of running away.

There is widespread confusion over the difference between adrenalin and noradrenalin; adrenalin is associated with feelings of stimulation, pleasure and excitement, but in fact it is the production of noradrenalin that produces these emotions. By contrast adrenalin produces feelings of fear and dread, such as those experienced before an examination or awaiting the results of some medical investigation; we feel like running away. When we are in control of a situation, when our perception of a situation is that the demands on us are not too great, we produce noradrenalin in greater amounts; when we are *not* in control, when we feel the demands are too great for us, we produce greater amounts of adrenalin, leading to the physical symptoms of fast-beating heart, feelings of breathlessness, sweating palms and dry mouth.

Teacher training should if possible incorporate some work on ways in which stress and tension can be anticipated and suggestions should be given for countering the effects, both physical and mental, on the teacher. It is important for everyone to look at their own working environment and try to instigate ways in which issues can be resolved with as little stress as possible. It is also important to remember that for some people stress is a stimulating and exciting experience. They feel that the demands they face are challenging and that they can handle them, so the consequent stress is, for them, good stress. Two people facing the same situation can experience two very different outcomes, one seeing the situation as challenging and a positive stress situation, the other finding the situation so stressful as to be unbearable.

Time Management

Part of the way in which we view any situation is the result of learned behaviour; in other words one individual will know that in a particular situation they cannot cope, they do not have the capacity to meet the demands, whereas another person will know that his or her capacity to deal with a situation far exceeds any demands that will be imposed. This 'demands and capacities' model is one which many teachers experience on a daily basis within their working environment. Activities which will make you feel relaxed should if possible be built into daily life, for example spending a few minutes quietly at the beginning of the school day alone in the classroom. It is often easy to feel that there is no time for such an activity but often time can be found. Time management and task prioritisation are key points in the battle to avoid undue stress and yet they are very difficult to achieve without help. Working with another person is a useful way of looking at issues that are of concern, and often the most recurring theme is lack of time. Something as simple as list making, a different method of filing, a memo or day book in which to write all tasks and carry forward those that have not been completed to the next day, will greatly help the administrative aspects of life that can become so overwhelming. Another effective method is to learn to say 'no', taking care that this decision does not simply shift the load from yourself to another colleague with equal workload and responsibilities. All too often if we were to examine our life in terms of a pie chart we would see that 75% of the circle is work related and only 25% pleasure related, yet of the 75% another 25% may be activities which have insidiously become part of our daily life and yet are activities which we have no real interest in or commitment to.

Teacher Action Research

Teacher 'action research' is receiving a lot of attention at the moment and this would surely be an area which would merit close attention with a view to empowering the teacher to make constructive changes to their personal and working environment. A workshop on time management is to be recommended as a productive way of spending in-service funds.

Chapter 4
How the Voice Works

For most people voicing is something that just happens, we open our mouths to verbalise our thoughts and voice occurs spontaneously. We think of something to say, we say it, and how it actually happens is a matter of some conjecture, if indeed we think of it at all. That is until something goes wrong and even then the mechanics of voice production are generally ignored and the most usually cited cure-all is either a hot drink with honey and lemon to 'soothe' your voice, or a period without talking to 'rest' the voice. More often the individual concerned struggles on, with faint cries of 'It will get better by itself, just give it a few days' and often that is exactly what does happen. The previously husky voice improves spontaneously and the individual heaves a sigh of relief and keeps on using their voice in exactly the same way...until the next time. Indeed if the individual concerned is a teacher he or she may have an opportunity for voice rest in the form of a half-term break or weekend and on Monday the voice seems a lot better, so back the teacher goes reporting to colleagues that all is now well...until the next time, as inevitably there will be a next time.

Misuse and Abuse of the Voice

It is difficult to think of any other injury that individuals pay as little attention to as voice injury. In general if we have muscle strain, back problems, a broken leg, or a sprained wrist we tend to say 'must be careful and not do that again' taking care when next in the same situation to avoid the problem. With voice disorders however, how often do we try to avoid the same situation? We may get into a smoky atmosphere or a dusty, noisy environment but rather than immediately making a fast exit in order to preserve our voice, we may rationalise it by saying, 'it would seem anti-social if I left, I will probably be fine after a night's sleep, perhaps I will get used to it after a while'. Rather than sit mutely by and not talk over a high noise level, we continue to shout over the band, and struggle home complaining of sore throats and voices that rasp perilously out of control from treble to bass. So why does this misuse and abuse of the voice continue to occur? If we had a large bruise on our leg we would hesitate to keep banging against it with the other leg, or to hit an injured arm with our fist. So what makes the voice so prone to self-inflicted vandalism? Part of the answer must lie in the fact that we cannot see the damage our vocal folds sustain and we thus remain supremely indifferent to any suggestion that damage is occurring. The voice that is slightly husky and breathy is often, as we have already said, referred to as 'sexy' rather than injured. Indeed many people prefer a vocal quality that is low in pitch, as an overly high pitch is sometimes perceived as shrill and unpleasant to listen to, so the 'injured' low voice can often pass without comment.

Perhaps a sign should be hung at the front of every school: 'You are now entering a voice watch zone', which would usefully serve to highlight the vocal problems endemic to school life.

The Mechanics of Voice

So what does happen within the larynx and why may it be of interest to readers? Certainly the authors are not advocating an intimate knowledge of the larynx as a pre-requisite for all professional voice users. A too scrupulous concern for what is happening within the larynx can sometimes inhibit vocal freedom and limit the expressivity of the voice which is very necessary for a professional voice user. At the same time the security of knowing that one's voice is efficient, effective and reliable is also essential, so it is important to be aware and knowledgeable about one's own voice; to begin to understand what it is or is not capable of. Some people are inherently good at sports, can run without tiring for miles and have enormous vitality while others wilt after the first half mile: so with the voice, some people are more vocally vulnerable than others, they cannot easily sustain extended periods of speech.

There is a need to recognise one's vocal limitations and avoid situations which exacerbate problems. Perhaps a useful analogy is that of driving a car. We may not be able to name each individual component in the engine, but we can listen to the noise of the engine and recognise by the engine noise when we need to change gear. If we see hazards ahead on our route we know how to steer around them. In the same way it is important to learn to listen and to hear when our voice is being strained so we can begin to recognise situations which are vocally hazardous. Having some basic knowledge of the mechanics of voice is rather like taking out an insurance policy. We can begin to identify trouble spots and avoid dangers, and as professional voice users it is imperative to protect one's most valuable asset. Only when we become aware of the needs of the voice can we begin the process of improving the vocally hazardous situation. It is important that there is information available to all, to allow changes to occur, both in the delivery of more training and increased vocal health education provision.

Each one of us has a voice that is unique, one that can be instantly identified as belonging to us by those whom we know. We can effect vocal change, in terms of altering volume, speed and pitch while still retaining the unique qualities that identify it as our voice. In this chapter we describe in considerable detail the structure of the larynx and the vocal process. This has been prompted by reports from course participants that information on how voice is produced helped them to modify particular patterns of behaviour and encouraged them to change abusive vocal habits.

Knowledge of the function and structure of the vocal process is not a pre-requisite of good voice but for many it does help to promote more effective use of voice and encourage vocal hygiene and conservation.

How Voice is Produced

Voice production is dependent on three different systems; the *respiratory system* responsible for the manner and pattern of breathing, the *phonatory system* responsible for how sound is produced at the level of the larynx and the *resonatory system* responsible for modification of this sound. These separate systems have been adapted to work together in the process of voice production although their primary biological purpose is of course to assist in life support. Without air we would die, without the closure of the vocal folds to sustain subglottic pressure we would find it much more difficult to lift heavy articles or push down, e.g. in defecation or childbirth, and without the epiglottis closing over the trachea, food or liquid would enter the lungs and we could choke. When this happens and food does 'go down the wrong way' the lungs try to expel it as quickly as possible and we cough violently.

When discussing the different systems it is clearer to differentiate one from another, although the systems are interdependent and voice is the result of a combined effort by all three. What must also be remembered is that these systems are directly affected by our posture. Virtually every bone in the body forms a joint or is connected to some other bone, allowing freedom of movement, but it also means that movement of one body part will affect another. The relationship between head, neck and back and what happens to the positioning of the spine and pelvis, will affect the rib cage and consequently respiration and voicing. For this reason when we think of voice work we need to consider the influence of the whole body, approaching voice in an holistic way rather than just attending to the sound in isolation.

The head is balanced on the top of the spine which is a flexible bony column that gives support to the trunk of the body. It is made up of twenty-four small bones called vertebrae, the top seven in the neck are called cervical vertebrae and it is the first of these, the atlas, that supports the skull. Below the neck are the twelve thoracic vertebrae (to which the ribs are attached) and five lumbar vertebrae. The ring-shaped vertebrae are separated by discs of cartilage. At the lower end of the spine is the pelvis, the bony structure that connects the spine with the legs, consisting of the hip bones on each side and the sacrum and coccyx behind. The bones of the pelvis protect the soft abdominal organs within them and of course support the base of the spine. The relationship between head, spine, pelvis and rib cage is, as we have said, critically important for efficient and effective voicing to occur.

What is Voice?

So what is 'voice', where does it come from and what is the process that changes silent thought into spoken word? Two absolute requirements for the production of sound of any kind are a source of energy and a vibrating structure. The primary source of energy for voice production is air provided by the lungs. They provide a smooth flow of air for the vibrating vocal folds to convert into sound. While the vocal folds are the principal source of sound, it is possible to constrict the vocal tract elsewhere along its length and create fricative noise, for example /s/ or /sh/, or indeed, a temporary blocking of the flow of air through the vocal tract followed by a sudden release of the air pressure can produce a mildly explosive sound for example /p/ and /t/. In continuous speech we produce both voiced (sounds produced at the level of the larynx) and unvoiced sounds. If we were to produce an analogue of the speech mechanism we would have a power supply which is breath, a vibrating element which is the vocal folds, a system of valves which is the vocal tract, and a filtering device which are the resonators.

Energy in the form of air from the lungs passes into the trachea and into the larynx. The larynx is the principal structure for producing a vibrating airstream and the vocal folds, which are part of the larynx, make up the vibrating elements. The vocal folds are long, smoothly rounded bands of muscle tissue which may be lengthened, shortened, tensed and relaxed as well as opened and closed across the airway. During normal breathing they are wide apart, the air stream is unimpeded and air flows in and out of the lungs in regular phases. For speech however, the vocal folds are closed or adducted to restrict the flow of air from the lungs, while at the same time air pressure below the folds increases and the vocal folds are literally blown apart releasing a puff of air into the vocal tract. This release of air results in a decrease of pressure below the folds and the elasticity of the tissue, plus the reduction of air pressure, allows them to snap back into their closed position ready to begin this cycle of vocal fold vibration again. In normal vowel production such vibrations occur at a rate of about 135 complete vibrations per second for men, about 235 vibrations per second for women and even more for children. This periodic interrupting of the air stream produces a vocal tone which is amplified within the pharyngeal, oral and nasal cavities and transformed through articulation of the lips, tongue and teeth and the result is meaningful speech sounds.

It can be seen from this brief description that for sustained speech, good breath support, plenty of air and flexible and relaxed respiratory muscles are needed, as are healthy and flexible vocal folds and free use of the resonators. If we look at each system in a little more detail we find three quite separate but interconnecting systems.

The Respiratory System

The process of breathing is called respiration and the main purpose of the respiratory system is to maintain life by carrying air into the lungs, where the exchange of the gases oxygen and carbon dioxide takes place. The respiratory system begins at the nose and mouth and ends with the alveoli in the lungs. The nasal and oral cavities (the nose and mouth) and the pharynx and larynx are known collectively as the upper respiratory tract, while the lower respiratory tract refers to the trachea, the bronchi and the lungs, which are housed within the bony thoracic or chest cavity. In addition to its role in respiration the upper respiratory tract functions in the process of swallowing, chewing, articulation, resonance and phonation, whereas the lower respiratory tract functions exclusively for the processes of breathing for life support and for the production of speech.

The respiratory tract has two parallel entrances, namely the nose and the mouth, through which air enters. These merge into a common tract or pharynx. The area within the pharynx immediately behind the nose (called the nasopharynx) and the area behind the mouth (called the oropharynx) are separated by a muscular valve, the soft palate, which when raised can close off one section from another, so that when we swallow, food and liquid does not escape through the nose. In the production of nasal consonants /n/, /m/ and /ng/ the soft palate is lowered to allow these sounds to be resonated in the nose.

The respiratory tract continues, passing through the larynx, through the open vocal folds into the trachea. The trachea divides into two branches: into the smaller bronchi that enter the lungs and ultimately into the even smaller alveoli. The pear-shaped lungs are contained within the bony rib cage, consisting of twelve pairs of ribs. The first pair of ribs are immobile, attached at the front to the sternum or breast bone and at the back to the spinal vertebrae. Pairs two to seven are similarly attached, but by synovial joints which allow a degree of rotation, while pairs eight to ten are attached to each other at the front by flexible cartilage and pairs eleven and twelve (commonly known as 'floating ribs') are fixed at the back to the spinal vertebrae but have no fixed attachment at the front. This arrangement of the ribs is important, because as the lungs are contained within this bony cage and linked to it by pleural and membranous tissue, alterations in the size and shape of the lungs when breathing in and out can be accommodated. This expansion is limited to the base of the lungs, as the top of the lungs are constrained by the fixed immobile ribs at the top of the rib cage. When we breathe in, the lungs expand and to accommodate their increase in size, the diaphragm (a large dome-shaped muscle which separates the cavity of the chest from that of the abdomen) contracts, so increasing the vertical space within the rib cage. At the same time there is an increase in the width of the chest from front to back due to the movement of the upper ribs, which moves the sternum upwards and forwards. The link that exists between the lungs and the rib cage means that expansion or contraction of the lungs, when breathing in or breathing out, will be mirrored by changes in the rib cage which will be either raised or lowered respectively, due to the movements of the intercostal muscles. For quiet respiration these changes are rarely noticed, the movement is so limited. It is only when we take in more air to support speech or song that we can readily identify the increased movement of the rib cage.

It is essential that the respiratory muscles are as flexible and efficient as possible in order to achieve this movement of the rib cage. The greater the expansion of the thoracic cavity the greater the volume of air that can be contained within the lungs and in order to achieve this the individual must rely on muscular flexibility and support.

There is a difference between quiet, at-rest 'breathing for life', which relies on equal phases of inspiration and expiration, and modified inspiration for the purposes of speech and song, where a quick intake and slow release of air is essential. It goes without saying that for the latter we need to have much more active control over respiration and as a consequence we need to be aware of the muscle groups involved. Even if the names are not particularly relevant for readers their position is important as their effectiveness in supporting breath is very much affected by posture and tension. Figures 3 and 4 below illustrate the position of the main respiratory muscles listed here.

Muscles of inspiration

These muscles are responsible for raising the rib cage and increasing the thoracic volume:

- The *diaphragm* – this large dome-shaped involuntary muscle is of great importance in respiration, playing the chief part in filling the lungs. During sleep and unconsciousness it maintains respiration under involuntary control.
- *External intercostal muscles* – act to control the amount of space between the ribs.
- *Accessory neck muscles* – act to help in elevation of the first and second ribs during inspiration.
- *Accessory back muscles* – contribute to rib movement during inspiration.
- *Accessory pectoral muscles* – contribute to expansion of the upper rib cage.

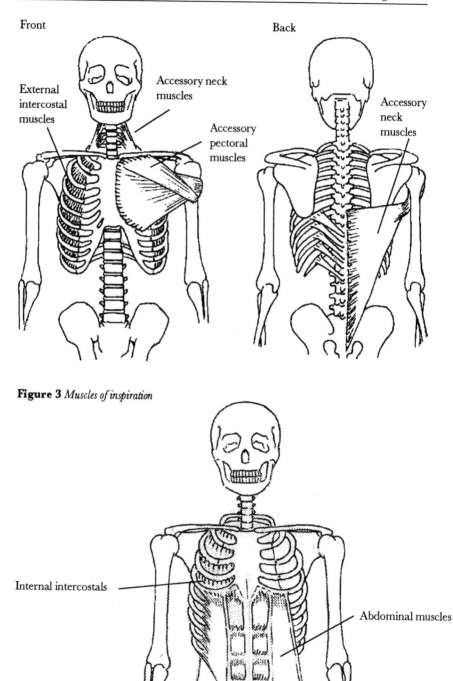

Figure 3 *Muscles of inspiration*

Figure 4 *Muscles of expiration*

Muscles of expiration

These muscles are responsible for lowering the rib cage and decreasing the thoracic volume.

- *Abdominal muscles* – responsible for a decrease in the dimensions of the thoracic cavity helping air to flow out of the lungs.
- *Back muscles* – act in aiding the ribs to depress.
- *Internal intercostal muscles* – act to help control the amount of space between the ribs.

When we look at the illustrations it is clear that for many their poor habitual posture will make it difficult to achieve optimum breath support and as a consequence the vocal folds will have much less support in terms of initiating and sustaining phonation. High shoulder posture, back and neck tension will all affect smooth muscle movement and for that reason, so many teachers find that one of the most critical first steps in achieving easier voicing is relaxation. Chapter 10 gives more information on how to achieve relaxation through specific relaxation exercises.

The Phonatory System

This is the system that actually produces the sound that we call voice and it consists of the larynx, or as it is more commonly known, the 'voice box', its muscles and ligaments and the hyoid bone, from which the larynx is suspended and to which several extrinsic laryngeal muscles are attached.

The principal biological function of the larynx is to act as a valve, preventing air from escaping from the lungs, preventing foreign substances from entering the larynx and expelling foreign substances that by-pass the epiglottis and threaten to enter the trachea.

The larynx is not a single structure, in fact it is made up of nine individual cartilages: three large single cartilages, the thyroid, cricoid and epiglottis, and three paired cartilages, the arytenoid, corniculate and cuneiform (see Figures 5a and 5b).

When thinking of cartilages we tend to think of something quite substantial but for readers who do not have any conception of the size of the larynx we should say at the outset that the larynx is in fact only 5 cm long. The vocal folds in men are between 15 and 20 mm in length, with those of women slightly shorter at approximately 9–13 mm long, so we are talking of a structure that is very small indeed.

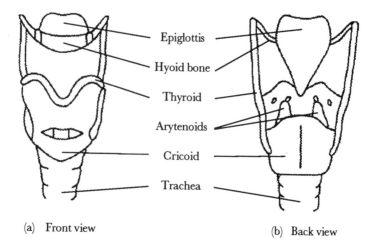

(a) Front view   (b) Back view

Figure 5: *Cartilages of the larynx*

The principal cartilages of the larynx are as follows.

The epiglottis

This is a broad leaf-shaped cartilage which is attached to the thyroid cartilage and projects upwards towards the tongue. The epiglottis changes position with tongue movements and alters the size and shape of the pharyngeal cavity.

The thyroid cartilage

This is the biggest cartilage, shaped like a shield, which forms most of the front and side walls of the larynx. It is composed of four quadrilateral plates fused at the front and this junction or angle of the thyroid is most visible in men and commonly called the 'Adam's apple'.

The cricoid cartilage

This cartilage is just below the thyroid cartilage and immediately above the trachea and attached to the thyroid cartilage by the cricotracheal ligament. Shaped like a signet ring it is narrow in front and broad behind and forms the base of the larynx.

Arytenoid cartilages

These small pyramid-shaped cartilages articulate with the cricoid cartilage via the cricoarytenoid joints. The arytenoids are the vocal gymnasts, they can in fact glide medially and laterally, rotate slightly and may also slide forwards and backwards but with restricted movement. Almost any combination of the above can occur simultaneously. Their importance in the production of voice lies in the fact that the vocal folds have an attachment to these cartilages via the vocal process so the specialised nature of their movements is essential in allowing the vocal folds to open and close with ease and thus produce changes in pitch. (See Figures 6a and 6b).

The vocal folds

The paired thyroarytenoid muscles make up the body of the vocal fold. The thyroarytenoid muscle has a superior portion, which forms the false vocal fold (mainly concerned with making a firm seal when swallowing occurs) and an inferior portion which forms the true vocal fold. In contrast to the red false folds the true vocal folds are white in colour. The space between the false and true vocal folds is known as the laryngeal ventricle and is well supplied with mucous glands thereby lubricating the vocal folds which are thus protected in part from the effects of friction. Within the larynx and the vocal tract the mucous membrane is usually moist, but dryness caused by infection, smoke and tension will noticeably affect the voice as the mucous membrane covering the vocal folds becomes dry. The very specialised structure of the vocal folds, composed of four different

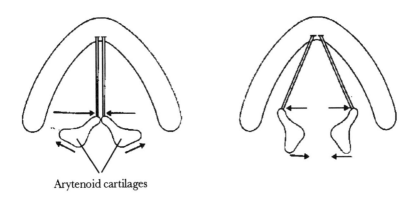

Arytenoid cartilages

(a) Closure of the vocal folds   (b) Opening of the vocal folds

Figure 6: *Schematic illustration of the movement of the arytenoid cartilages and consequent movement of the vocal cords*

tissue layers, each with different mechanical properties important for vibration, accounts for the amazing range and versatility of the voice.

The Resonatory System

The resonatory system consists of the chest, and the pharyngeal, oral and nasal cavities. The resonators above the larynx can alter in size, shape and tension through movement of the base of the tongue and the soft palate. In addition further modification can occur through contraction of the pharyngeal and extrinsic laryngeal muscles. While the larynx is obviously the primary contributor to the production of voice, without the acoustic influence of the resonators the voice would sound very thin indeed. When we think of the open mouth position adopted by singers and actors and contrast the sound with the sound we hear from speakers with limited mouth opening, we can hear the difference that resonance makes to a voice. Most of the quality and loudness characteristics that are associated with the voice are the result of the resonators. In the same way that the weak vibrations of the strings of a musical instrument are altered by the resonating body of the instrument, so the tone that is produced at the level of the larynx, the laryngeal buzz, is altered by the resonators. The airway above the larynx acts like an acoustic filter which can suppress or maximise some sounds as they pass through. Alterations can also occur in the configuration of the vocal tract by varying tongue positions, raising or lowering the soft palate and as an effect of the degree of relaxation or tension present. For the skilled professional voice user the effective use of the resonators can be a powerful tool in increasing the range and power of the voice and Chapter 10 will offer suggestions on exercises for the resonators.

Hormonal Changes

The specialised structure of the vocal folds is, as with the rest of the body, influenced by hormonal, endocrinological and ageing changes. Hormonal changes account for the voice breaks and uncertain pitch that occur in the male voice at puberty, where the vocal folds increase in length and thickness. For women endocrinological changes during menstruation and pregnancy may increase the chances of fluid retention and consequent swelling of the vocal folds. Similarly the menopause signals a reduction of ovarian hormones and often an accompanying swelling of the vocal folds, in both instances leading to a deterioration in vocal quality and huskiness. For many professional singers clauses in their contracts allow them to withdraw from performances during menstruation. Studies have shown that premenstrual changes in the vocal folds lead to changes which contribute to a perception by the listener of vocal harshness or roughness. As with any musical instrument, if the free edges of the vocal folds are damaged, swollen, dry or lacking in tension then the resultant sound will be less than adequate. Typically, swollen vocal folds will give a husky, breathy quality, the free edges do not meet cleanly to vibrate easily together due to the swelling, and often air escapes leading to the breathy sound. Equally, damage such as vocal nodules or polyps, often cited as problems by 'pop' singers who have strained their voices due to the lack of proper training, will affect voice quality adversely. It is certainly important that individuals learn to recognise even slight vocal changes and take care of their voice. Women should be particularly aware that during their monthly cycle their voices may be vulnerable.

Effects of Ageing

Changes due to ageing should also be recognised; changes in pitch level and pitch range accompany growth changes in boys' voices and changes in puberty. Changes also occur due to the ageing process (Luchsinger and Arnold 1965) and while change in pitch range that may accompany increasing age are not well documented there seems to be a trend towards a decrease in range with increasing age. Laryngeal cartilages calcify, a process that begins quite early in adulthood and starts sooner and is more complete in men than in women. By old age the changes are quite extensive in both sexes and certainly the vocal folds of old people look very different from those of younger adults. There is frequently greyish or yellowish discoloration of the tissue, loss of mass and a residual gap on vocal fold adduction.

Specific tissue structure changes occur within the folds, so that the cover undergoes alteration, epithelial thickening is observed (that is changes occur in the upper cellular layer of the vocal fold) and changes in the underlying connective tissue result in looser linkage of the epithelium to the deeper tissues. The elastic fibres of the vocal ligaments break down and become thinner while the mucous glands degenerate, resulting in less adequate lubrication of the vocal fold surface and probable changes in the biomechanical properties of the superficial epithelium. As with other muscles the laryngeal muscles are prone to atrophy, which means that there are fewer muscle fibres in each muscle and in addition the surviving fibres tend to be thinner and to show significant degenerative changes. It is possible that these changes result from disturbances of the blood supply.

As the vocal folds become less elastic, bowing can occur, the vocal folds cannot vibrate along their full length leading to a weak breathy note. This seems to be particularly a problem with older men leading to a thinner higher voice, while women, as we have said, tend to have slightly thicker more swollen vocal folds in older age, limiting their range. As well as changes within the larynx, ageing brings about changes within the lungs which deteriorate with increasing age and of course smoking accelerates this deterioration. Reduction of the mobility of the thoracic cage occurs, the ribs become less mobile and with advanced age the lungs and bronchi shrink and sink to a lower position in the thorax, while the sensitivity of the airway is reduced and coughing is less likely to occur. Physical activity will prevent noticeable deterioration in respiration and of course it is important to avoid pollutants as these will affect the elastic recoil of the lungs. With declining respiratory function, voice quality is affected due to lack of breath support. If however an individual pays attention to postural, respiratory and vocal health they can maintain a voice that sounds much younger than their chronological age.

There are therefore changes in the sound of the voice and alterations to the larynx which accompany ageing but it would be inappropriate to suggest that all the changes are the result of alterations to the laryngeal cartilages. Indeed it may be that the loss of flexibility within the vocal folds means that glottal closure becomes less complete and less stable and results in a sound which is perceived as being somewhat rough and perhaps breathy. This quality is one that we associate with the older individual.

Chapter 5
Voice as a Physical Skill

When we use the voice to communicate, it is not just the larynx and the organs of speech that are involved in the process but the whole body. Chapter 4 highlighted the many muscles used in the production of the sound. In addition to these muscles the spine and the relationship of the pelvis, rib cage, head, neck and shoulder girdle to the spine, have a significant effect upon the voice. Our sense of physical self is generally not as accurate as we like to think it is. If you ask someone to close their eyes and using their hands, indicate the width of their hips, head or waist, or the length of their foot, you will find that they generally overestimate the size. We also often mistakenly think we are taller or shorter than we actually are, even when we judge height in comparison with other people we know well. Some people have little concept of themselves within space; they duck unnecessarily when passing through doorways and when asked to explore the space behind themselves, agree that this is an area they do not generally consider they inhabit. We also tend to use the same spatial levels repeatedly. An exercise we have used to great effect is to ask a group to imagine themselves in a personal glass sphere and to use their hands and feet to touch and explore the outer limits of it. Adults get a great deal of pleasure from this exercise, reporting that it opens up a 'new' dimension to them.

Vocal Culture

We hear it said that as a society we have become very cerebral. We 'live' in our heads and our language has become a means of expressing ideas and conveying information rather than the physical and emotional language of 'less sophisticated' societies whose cultures are more vocally liberated and who have maintained a strong tradition of song, dance and story-telling in their communities. Loud voices accompanied by expansive physical gestures tend to be considered flamboyant or excessive in certain Western countries. Lack of voice/body connection and a poor sense of being in touch with our bodies combined with a lack of understanding of the links between body and voice, can limit our ability to recognise the early warning signals of a voice in trouble.

Body Balance

Many of our vocal problems are caused by a lack of balance in body alignment. This balance can be altered by something as simple as a pair of high-heeled shoes that tip the natural balance of the pelvis and this in turn can have an effect upon the spine, head and shoulders and ultimately the voice.

The Spine

The spine reaches from the head to the coccyx. It is made up of the vertebrae which are bones that connect with each other. Between each vertebra are the intervertebral discs, cartilages that separate one vertebra from another and provide a cushion. The spine has a certain amount of flexibility and it also has natural curves. The flexibility of the spine and its curves allow us to move easily and smoothly and to jump and land without injuring ourselves, the curves in our spines absorb the shock of jolting and landing. The spine, most importantly, shields the spinal cord and the nerve fibres come through the openings between the vertebrae. Often, when we think of correcting our alignment we think of 'straightening the spine' but we need to retain the spinal curves and, without over-exaggerating or straightening them, we need the spine to feel long. Figure 7 shows the necessary curves in the neck, thoracic and lumbar regions of the spine. At the top of the spine is the head, positioned on what is called the atlanto-occipital joint, the joint between the top vertebra and the bottom of the skull.

The Head

We always ask participants in our workshops what they think the head weighs. The answers range from the very light 2 or 3 pounds to the much more accurate 12 to 15 pounds, which often amazes people. An exercise we find very illustrative is to 'pair' people off and to get one of the pair to lie on the floor, the other sits at his or her head and gently eases tension in the shoulder area by massaging.

Figure 7: *The spinal curve*

After assuring the 'prone' individual that they will not drop their head, one person carefully takes the weight of the other's head in their hands. To begin with the head usually feels very light because the individual on the floor is using the large muscles of the neck to hold the weight. Once they trust the 'holder' enough they may gradually give up control and when this happens the holder begins to feel the true weight of the head and will find that they can move the head gently from side to side without interference from the 'owner'.

Practical suggestions

An easy way to experience the weight of the head for yourself is to lie on the floor and to lift your head about an inch off the ground. Feeling the stress this places on the muscles of the neck gives an idea of the benefits of balancing the head on the top of the spine in an effortless manner, leaving all the muscles of the neck, jaw and shoulders stress free. It will also allow the jaw to move freely, not restricting the movement needed to produce voice and speech.

An excellent exercise for developing awareness in the top of the neck is the 'nodding dog' or 'marionette'. This exercise involves isolating the small muscles that allow the head to rock gently in a smooth, weightless manner, rather like the movement of the toy dogs found on car dash-boards that have a head attached by a large spring to the body. As the car moves the head wobbles – a very similar movement is seen in films of the *Thunderbirds*.

1.   In order to practise the exercise, which can be done sitting or standing, it is important to first feel length in the neck and then to exercise the large muscles by drawing imaginary floor to ceiling lines with the nose. Start these lines at the right shoulder and move across to the left 'using' the nose as a pen. This exercise allows you to stretch and release the uppermost neck muscles, which contract in stress.

2.   Still using the nose as a pen draw a fluid figure of eight, firstly in the normal upright manner and secondly as if it were lying on its side, so that you move across to your right side and then through the centre point to the left side.

3.   Imagine a column of water is spouting up the spine and the head is floating on the top of it. Feel the weightlessness of the head.

4.   Allow the head to bounce gently on the spine as if you were a marionette. Make all moves in slow motion first.

5.   Lastly, making sure the jaw is not clenched, try gentle 'Yes' nods, then 'No' nods and finally try to use both in a 'Nodding dog' movement. These take some practice but they give a very useful awareness to the area of the body most involved in the 'fight or flight' positions.

Unlocking the Knees

An area of the body that is not initially associated with voice is the knee area. Most of us brace our knees in order to steady ourselves, particularly when we are under stress. The person unused to the experience of public speaking or performing often remarks 'My knees were shaking' or 'I went weak at the knees.' When the knees are locked, a lower abdominal tension is created which interferes with diaphragmatic movement. In order for the breath to flow in and out of the body it is important to stand in a balanced and open

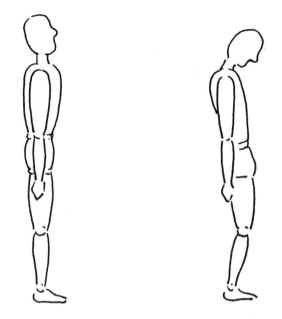

Figure 8a *Overcorrect position*   **Figure 8b** *Slumped position*

manner, with the knees released and flexed, the feet in contact with the floor and the body arranged around the spine with the feeling that it is lengthened and wide.

The term 'lengthen' is often used in connection with posture. This comes from the *Alexander technique* which teaches the need to gently oppose the force of gravity which seems intent on 'squashing' us downward and inwards. The word 'oppose' is preferable to 'fight' because it does not bring with it images of overcorrection. Amongst teachers it is as common to find overcorrected regimented posture as it is to find slumped, contracted posture. What is less common is the open, lengthened and wide 'ideal'. It could be said that the teacher's posture is a measure of the way in which the stresses of contemporary teaching life are handled by the individual concerned. Some seem bowed by the volume of work and the seemingly insurmountable pressures, others take on the 'struggle' – literally – with chin thrust forwards and shoulders braced (see Figures 8a and 8b).

The Importance of Eye Level

Another underestimated physical aspect is the effect that eye level has on the body and therefore, the voice. The shy child or intimidated individual often avoids eye contact. With the lowered head comes a depressed sternum; this results in a lack of openness in the ribs, which seem to slump towards the hip area, and the result of this is a shallow breath. (The depressed individual often manifests a similarly shallow breathing pattern which in turn produces a monotonous vocal quality.) The lowered eyes of the shy or depressed individual can be mistaken as signalling a shifty or devious person. The opposite of this is a rigidly fixed focus which tends to correspond to locked neck, clenched jaw and stiffly held shoulders, leading to an enormous amount of un-useful tension which limits the free exchange of breath, and produces a vocal quality that is often strident and can appear aggressive. This position limits peripheral vision as the eyes, being fixed, do not scan, but look fixedly ahead. The assumption made of such a physical posture is that the individual has either an aggressive approach, or is constantly on their guard. They may often appear to be startled and because of the rigidity this position creates, the voice produced is strident, unfriendly and lacks flexibility and possibly warmth.

When the eye level is the result of open and balanced alignment the eyes are able to see the periphery, and therefore the individual is able to function within their world in an aware and integrated manner. None of us produce all the symptoms of these extremes, but the example is made clearer by their polarisation.

It is important also to mention that the rib cage, which is attached to the spine and which houses the lungs, becomes depressed when the spine loses its natural length. This usually results in the slumping forward of the shoulders so that the entire 'front' of the body closes downward and inward and space for breathing to occur easily, as well as the elasticity of the ribs, is lost.

The proper alignment of the body allows it to work harmoniously and without creating unnecessary tensions. Consider for instance the tension created when the head, which as we have mentioned weighs between 12 and 15 pounds, is carried in front of the shoulders rather than by being balanced on the top of the spine. If 14 pounds of wood were to be carried comfortably, it would, quite naturally, be held close to the body rather than at arm's length. The head, however, is often held away from the body at the end of an extended neck. The effect on the muscles of the neck, jaw and shoulders is considerable and as we have already seen, there is a direct link between these muscles and the larynx.

The Child's Ability to Shout

Most primary school children in the playground are able to scream and shout during play time without losing their voices. There are a

number of reasons for this; firstly they tend to have natural alignment, secondly they are playing so that their activities are free of
harmful negative tensions (though no one would deny the positive
tension involved in exuberant play) and thirdly they are generally
using the whole chest and *releasing* the outgoing breath rather than
holding it. There are, of course, exceptions to these generalisations, as
some children can develop nodules or polyps on the vocal folds
through improper use but they are in the minority.

Secondary school children present a very different picture. The
difference between the open and proud posture of the average 6-
year-old and that of the average 16-year-old is considerable. In our
workshops when we ask teachers to demonstrate the posture of the
average children in the class, boys are portrayed very differently
from girls. What we see in the boys takes two forms – either the
assumed confidence of the tight high-shouldered swagger, or a
slumped spine body position with a concave chest, low eye level,
with the head carried in front of the shoulders. Girls are often
portrayed as slumping forward with arms folded across the chest,
or in some cases around the waist. In both boys and girls the significant similarity is the weight distribution which is usually across
one, not two, feet or hips, resulting in a loss of space between the
lower ribs and the hips, limiting the ribs' ability to increase breath
capacity and support the voice through expansion of the lower
lung area.

Changes in Adolescence

Just why this change from easy open posture and alignment to tight
contracted or slumped stance occurs in the adolescent and in some
cases the pre-adolescent years is a subject open to much discussion. It
is obviously the result of a number of factors. As children grow, particularly if they have a sudden 'growth spurt', they may temporarily lose
some motor control and can appear ungainly, for instance they may
walk into objects or stub their toes. We also know that the way they
feel about themselves and their developing bodies can make them feel
vulnerable and exposed. Much of the body language seen is an
attempt either to protect themselves by withdrawing from society and
making themselves inconspicuous by occupying as little space as
possible, or to assume a confidence they do not feel by lifting the
shoulders, thrusting the jaw and taking up a greater amount of physical space. During this period, holding eye contact in everyday
communication is extremely difficult as some young people cannot

bring themselves to confront adults, so their eye level tends to be lowered and this produces the head–neck alignment that develops a slumped spine and results in shallow breathing (see Figure 9).

Figure 9: *Slumped adolescent posture*

In some teenagers it is possible to see the development of the use of head, neck and jaw in conveying the body language of either aggression or fear. We are familiar with the way we perceive the threatening body language of the forward thrust jaw or the low eye levels found in the fearful and insecure. Our language has assimilated our attitudes to voice and body language; we say, 'Be brave, take it on the chin', 'Keep your chin up', 'You look as if you are carrying the world on your shoulders'. We also talk about 'Taking a deep breath' and say 'Grin and bear it' in difficult situations when we need courage. We talk of 'Being lost for words' or 'Speechless' when in situations that promote frustration, of 'Being so angry I could not speak' and in cases of sadness, 'Having a lump in my throat'.

What produces this neck, shoulder and head reaction to fear and anger is a basic human instinct that has been with us since our earliest days. It has been called the 'fight or flight' instinct by anthropologists and the Alexander teachers refer to it as the 'startle' effect.

Adulthood

By the time we reach adulthood, most of us have gained at least a little confidence, or at least a working strategy for dealing with our lack of confidence, so we are less likely to develop new posture problems. The problem is that we seldom correct or change the habits of our adolescence, the postural and movement pattern has been set and it is within this pattern that we operate. Even when we do try to re-align ourselves, the body 'prefers' the old pattern, in fact it rejects the new posture as wrong because it identifies and is comfortable with the old habitual position. For this reason it is a very good idea, should you suspect posture may be a contributing factor in a voice problem, to seek advice and to work with the help of an 'outside eye'. There are many people who can help from physiotherapists, osteopaths, Alexander technique teachers and yoga teachers. It is important to find someone who is qualified to work with the body therapeutically. It is not an over-rigid, overcorrected posture that is required but a balanced one. Whoever helps you needs to know that your body is individual and needs to find its own balance. It is easy to become over-erect which creates unwanted and unnecessary tensions, and this is almost more harmful than the slumped posture. For this reason the advice on alignment offers general principles but we strongly advise you to find a way of working in a 'hands on' manner, if you possibly can. An objective eye is most helpful and to begin with a professionally trained teacher is recommended. If however you have to work alone, some of the following suggestions may be useful.

Some Useful Physical Strategies

Video

No matter how many times we may be told by others that our posture needs correction, because it is habitual and therefore natural to us, we often find it very difficult to 'step outside ourselves' and see ourselves as others see us. One of the great advantages we have is the opportunity to see ourselves on video. If you know you need to work on posture but do not really understand what adjustments need to be made, ask a friend to video you, preferably when you are not conscious of the camera. This can be rather a shock, because we generally watch ourselves very critically and with a degree of vanity, when objectivity is what we really need to develop. (A mirror is useful but does not offer us the profile or back view.) If you get the opportunity, notice the head/shoulder relationship and the natural but unexaggerated curves in the lower back and thoracic spine. Notice also whether you carry the head forward or correctly balanced on the top of the spine. This exercise is best undertaken individually or in very small groups who are happy to take suggestions from each other.

Spot reminders

A very successful way of re-patterning the physical memory is to use the simple method of applying small coloured spots to strategic points around the home, office or classroom. For example, should you want to remind yourself to relax your shoulders, place a spot on the wall near the telephone and in easy view so that when you are speaking you see the spot and immediately check the shoulder position. Posture often suffers if the phone is being held between shoulder and head, while the hands are involved in other activities such as paging through phone books, or looking up references; even cooking can be done while speaking on the phone. Other useful positions for spots are on the fridge door, or the edge of your VDU or typewriter, on the steering wheel of your car, on the edge of the classroom blackboard, or the school piano.

Effort levels

When our levels of stress are high, we are less able to assess our use of effort, which for most of us is a difficult task even when we are at our most relaxed. Most of the time we assume that we operate at either high or low levels, depending on whether we are having a good day or a bad one. It is very useful to be able to gauge our physical and vocal levels so that we can expend energy appropriately and not waste it unnecessarily – stress is tiring and unproductive. The efficient use of energy and effort depends on developing awareness of the degrees of effort necessary for the task and matching the effort to the demand.

Suggested exercise

An easy exercise that helps to familiarise us with our effort levels is to shake hands in pairs. Person A asks person B to rate their own handshake on a scale of 1 to 10. If for example they rate it at 7, A then asks B to shake at level 3 or 9, then return to 7, go down to 4 and so on until they have established a graduated scale of effort. The partners then change over and repeat the exercise. The practical application to voice is very useful as many teachers, once they have mastered the discipline, can make a conscious decision to use a lower level of vocal onset or attack, by sounding an /ah/ vowel with varying degrees of energy. This exercise can then be extended using a familiar classroom phrase or instruction, for example 'put your books away now'.

Ask for an inset day designed to look at alignment

Many industrial and commercial businesses are investing in postural training because of the enormous number of working days lost through back injury. The money spent on a physiotherapist, osteopath, Alexander teacher or similar physical therapist coming into school to advise on individual and group needs is never wasted, but is seldom done, because curriculum needs always tend to take precedence over the needs of the teaching staff.

Chapter 6
Communication

Professional voice users, the group to which teachers belong, are, in the jargon of the day, in the 'communication business' but sometimes the skills of 'getting the message across' have either never been learned or else have been given a low priority. This is perhaps not surprising in the face of the current teacher workload and indeed the heavy academic pressures that teachers have to face before qualifying. It is however one of the most essential skills for a teacher; how often do we remember a teacher from our past, not for what she or he actually taught us, but for the enthusiasm and energy they brought to the lesson? Often this influenced our subject choice and it is perhaps salutary to think of how few teachers in our school life we remember who had this ability to share their enthusiasm for their subject with us and to really communicate. Most teachers are enthusiastic about their subject, but some are unable to share that enthusiasm with pupils because their communication skills are limited. This chapter suggests some aspects of communication and self-presentation skills that teachers might find of benefit.

What exactly do we mean by communication? The process of communication can be divided broadly into two areas: verbal and non-verbal. When we think of verbal communication we think generally of speech, but speech as we perceive it is composed of several interdependent elements which are outlined below.

Language

The ability to convert ideas into words is fundamental to the communication process. There is no point in having the most wonderful appreciation of one's subject if you find it impossible to find words with which to transmit these ideas fluently and imaginatively to others and in a form relevant to the audience. Effective speech is the process of getting an idea from one mind to another accurately and persuasively. We have all been to lectures and heard the 'woolly talker', the individuals who know exactly what they mean – but they are the only ones who understand.

This is where the choice of words, their arrangement and the way in which they are expressed are the tools that will achieve this end most effectively. Language lives, changes and responds to different social and cultural mores, and certainly the fact that the English language has the capacity to change and to grow creatively, by absorbing vocabulary from other cultures and countries, has made it the dynamic language that it is today. In France, where the use of grammatically correct spoken and written language is intimately connected to nationalistic identity, there was an attempt in 1995 to ban certain foreign words, mainly English and American, from advertisements and public pronouncements. The attempt was ill conceived and subjected to a certain amount of ridicule. English has always had the capacity to take and make its own vocabulary from elsewhere. This is what allows language to grow and survive in a truly pragmatic way.

So the choice of words will convey, more or less effectively, the meaning to the listener but the way in which the words are expressed will affect the impact the message has on the speaker. Within the area of verbal communication we need to consider other parameters of speech, namely articulation, voice quality and vocal variety which underpin the way words are expressed.

Articulation

Articulation is the way in which we produce speech sounds in order to make language intelligible to the listener. The clarity of speech depends on the accuracy of the movements of the articulators; tongue, lips, jaw and teeth. The current vogue for a lack of precise articulation often leads to a loss of understanding; we do not completely understand what the speaker is saying and if we do not understand we tend to 'switch off'. Positioning plays an important role in aiding understanding as it is often particularly difficult for pupils when a teacher, whose articulation is not very precise, stands with their back to the class, writing notes on the blackboard and giving information at the same time. We do not always recognise how much we rely on lip reading to aid our understanding, but a useful exercise is to monitor how much we look at a speaker to aid our understanding. Deliberately look away from a speaker and judge how much added listening effort is needed to understand the speaker when we cannot rely on facial expression, body posture and articulatory movements to help us. If we cannot see a speaker we often feel that we need to listen harder.

There seems to be a general perception that clear, precise articulation is somewhat outdated, decidedly unfashionable, and little value is currently placed on defined articulation. This is not to advocate a return to the rather clipped articulation of the 1940s and 1950s that black and white films so faithfully reproduce, but it is possible to be aware of articulation and to see it as a very useful tool, helping to maintain the class's interest and as an effective aid when teaching. With clarity of articulation there is less need for repetition and as a result there is less need to use the voice unnecessarily. The muscularity of speech is never fully present if the speaker is not mentally committed to the word, on the other hand the enthusiastic teacher with a need to share ideas rarely has a problem being understood. Only when the synchronisation of thought and word occurs is language wholly energised. A return to the energised use of consonants, particularly the explosive consonants, /b/, /d/ and /g/ (voiced) and /p/, /t/ and /k/ (un-voiced) brings a dynamic to language and produces the physical and vocal movement inherent in words like bubble, hop, tap, bounce, kick, drag, slap and giggle.

Often in our culture too much obvious commitment to the dynamics of words is seen as flamboyant, over-assertive or arrogant. Some individuals feel they would be making themselves vulnerable by such 'overstated' voice use or that they would appear pedantic. In truth it is possible to appear all these things if articulation is pushed or unrelated to the meaning behind it.

There is something exciting about listening to an individual who is inspired by an idea and you only have to watch children 'hang on' to the words of an effective story-teller to know the power that language has to access the imagination of the listener. The speech of young children is full of the sounds that they hear around them – 'splash', 'swoosh', 'ping', 'gurgle', the sounds of whistles, explosions and the noise of cars, motorbikes, aeroplanes and machinery. Of course those who read comics add the expletives such as 'Kapow!', 'Zap!' and 'Gadoom!' to their vocabulary, and when making these sounds they use the muscularity of speech in an uninhibited and joyous way. This playful use of the articulatory organs helps them to develop vocal and verbal muscle and imbue sound with an energy that, regrettably, adults often lose. Practise, using carefully selected verse, can help to maintain the imaginative use of words; and adults too can explore their own use of language through prose and verse.

The use of the final consonant is essential in the delivery of any information and therefore critical in teaching. Conversational speech that is relaxed and delivered to one or two people does not require a deliberate weighting of consonants, but once the speech becomes public, that is to say to an audience or class, there is a need to emphasise the consonants in order to aid definition and increase audibility, for example the final consonant in the word 'find' needs to be heard or the word could be confused with 'fine'. Male teachers should be aware that lip reading is made more difficult by the addition of facial hair from beards or moustaches, so for the more hirsute teacher, articulatory precision is even more important.

Voice

Voice works on many levels; firstly, it goes without saying, it makes speech audible, but it also gives definition to what is being said in many different ways, notably through changes in intonation and vocal pitch, alterations in pace, through the use of pause, by putting stress on particular syllables within words and by emphasising certain words in sentences.

Other Vocal Parameters

If we look at these vocal parameters individually we can better identify them.

Intonation

Intonation can be said to provide a vocal blueprint; it describes the way in which a specific voice alters during speech. When we ask a question, for example, we use an intonation pattern that is very different from that used when we express an opinion. When we are in a situation in which we feel under-confident we often resort to the questioning vocal tune because we feel it produces an impression of politeness and conciliation. This tune can often be heard in the voices of teachers who work with pre-primary and infant school children, as it does not sound threatening or aggressive. When used inappropriately however, it can give the impression of being uncertain and tentative. The other extreme is the continual use of the 'definite statement tune' which is often used by those in high status or authoritative positions and generally used by newscasters, as it is perceived as being 'the truth' and not to be questioned. While this is a confident and assertive tune, if used inappropriately it can make students feel that there is no space or opportunity for asking questions or sharing ideas.

The benefits of understanding the intricacies of human perceptions and assumptions are obvious, particularly as teachers are continually interrelating with students and other members of staff on a verbal and vocal level. Particular emphasis should be given to this aspect of vocal behaviour when in an interview situation or in the ever-increasing appraisal situations. More and more business and industrial courses are concentrating on the importance and power of paralinguistic skills. These are skills fundamental to the teacher's professional role, but ones which to date receive little attention during training.

Each language and dialect has an inherent tune that expresses emotion and attitude that we become aware of fairly quickly. Even if we were not native English speakers we could listen to an exchange and make an educated guess as to whether the speakers were having an argument, exchanging pleasantries or asking questions, just by the way in which the individual voices were moving through the pitch range.

Pitch

The pitch of the voice will often carry the emotional content of speech. When we become excited or stressed vocal pitch often rises and the voice becomes shrill. In the same way, when we are frightened or very angry we may literally 'lose our voice'; we cannot do more than whisper. Often individuals will use a very low vocal pitch when they are attempting to maintain control or when they are in a situation in which they want to appear more authoritative. If we look at female executives, women in authority, teachers or women who are in competition with men, we find that many have adopted what could be called a gender-neutral vocal quality: not too high-pitched and not too light in terms of resonance, yet not so deep as to appear masculine. Women will often try and consciously lower their pitch as they feel it gives them more status and as a consequence what they say; will carry more weight this is not to be recommended as it can often damage the voice. Judicious use of pause and changes in intonation can often achieve the same effect. Underpitching the voice in this way also limits its range and results in an uninteresting, limited vocal quality.

Pace and rate

Alterations in pace or in the speed at which we speak greatly influence the way in which the listener interprets what we are saying. If we are excited and enthusiastic we tend to speak more quickly. Think of speakers you know who speak very quickly; there is a sense of urgency behind what they are saying. This device can often be used in meetings where the fast talker virtually 'steam-rollers' the meeting as the rest of the group has no chance to interrupt and scarcely time to assimilate what is being said. At the opposite end of the spectrum, if we are uncertain about facts or simply unsure as to what we actually think about an issue, we often speak quite slowly and hesitantly, frequently introducing fillers like 'er' and 'um', so we appear to weigh up each word. Often this slow delivery can be thought of as demonstrating uncertainty and indeed the speaker can sometimes take so long to make their point that despite the validity of the statement, people have switched off and often disregard what they are saying. On the other hand it can also be seen as evidence of the speaker's commitment to an idea or an opinion and a sign of their confidence in expressing it. The advantage of using a fairly slow delivery rate is that it allows the speaker time to think ahead and make sure that he or she has complete control of what he or she is saying. Faster speech often does not allow the speaker to do this and spontaneous or 'off the cuff' speech tends to be faster, although on occasions this may be the result of anxiety and can result in gabbled speech. Politicians tend to use the device of slow speech which allows them less chance of unwittingly blurting out an unreasoned opinion. In order however to maintain the interest of the listener, it is important to allow the content to determine the pace of delivery, otherwise the predictability of pace becomes monotonous and unrelated to intention.

The vocal blueprint

A part of the overall picture we have of people is provided by the voice. This is most easily demonstrated by the visual picture you have of people you do not see. The radio announcer, for example, is wholly represented by their voice. This representation is partly dependent on the sound of the voice – the vocal pitch, tone and quality of the resonance, partly on the accent of the speech and partly on the content and manner of delivery. A number of research projects (Farb 1973) have explored reactions to the 'disembodied voice' and found that listeners make a very definite assumption about the speaker's age, physical appearance, including height and weight, the educational background, family background and class, status, residential area, political persuasion, level of assertiveness and intelligence. Similarly when we speak to unfamiliar people on the phone we react in the same way, we make instinctive judgements. Various subtle messages, conscious and unconscious, are conveyed by the tone of the voice and it is quite possible for the words to be 'saying' one thing and the voice to be 'saying' another. We have all had the experience of asking someone how they are and they respond with 'fine' and yet we know they are not. Feelings of lack of self-esteem, tension, tiredness, sadness or boredom are all reflected in the voice. In the same way voice quality is very influential in the impressions we give and receive.

Vocal quality

There are certain vocal qualities which are perceived as more friendly than others, a speaker with warm 'mellow' tones seems to be interpreted as someone who can be trusted, who is sincere and friendly, while a 'harsher' more forced voice quality can appear aggressive and threatening. The voice plays an important role in the interview situation, the advantages for the individual candidate who is able to conceal nervousness by a relaxed vocal quality and the disadvantages for another who presents with a voice that rises in pitch, seems to 'crack' and needs to be cleared constantly, are plain.

In the classroom pupils make assumptions like everyone else. The male or female teacher who is unable to control a class often cites their voice as the cause. 'My voice isn't strong, so they don't think I mean what I say', 'They say they can't hear me at the back of the class, so they just keep talking.' Male teachers often find maintaining discipline easier than women teachers and some of this can in part be attributed to their vocal quality. It has been noticeable that several male teachers with fairly light voice quality, who we have seen on courses, have been the ones who have complained that they could not easily gain and keep the attention of the class. They reported that they had to spend a lot of time forcing their voices to produce a louder, deeper sound and often resorted to shouting, and as a consequence they developed vocal problems. Many teachers who have problems being vocally commanding resort to shouting and the effect of this is often that, far from appearing to be *in* control, they are indeed perceived as having *lost* control. Pupils often complain that a teacher 'always sounds angry and aggressive' but when questioned further this can be due less to the content of what is said and more to the quality of vocal delivery.

Modulation

Modulation of the voice is an important aspect of how we communicate, how we 'get a message' across. Teachers often complain that their voices lack interest or modulation, they feel the voice is contained within a very narrow range and that it does not move in response to thought or word, they feel it should be 'modulated'. Modulation, however, is a word much used and often misunderstood. It often suggests (erroneously) a technical changing and varying of the voice, without any regard to the thought that produced it. Movement of the voice through a series of cadences without reason produces a sound just as unconnected to mind and action as a dull monotonous voice. Ideally the voice should respond to changes in thought which then become reflected in a variety of subtle nuances. If, however, tension or stress levels are high, it is likely that this natural delivery will be inhibited. When the individual is relaxed and at ease the voice moves effortlessly and naturally through its range and the movement reinforces the intention of the language rather than distracting from it.

Emphasis

Of course, there are aspects to be considered such as pause, pace and stress but their use or lack of use is usually an indicator of how open or happy the teacher is about using the voice freely and responsively rather than being due to a lack of a specific technique. Emphasis is always present when a speaker has the 'need' to speak. You only have to listen to a group of enthusiasts debating a subject close to their hearts to understand this.

Pauses

Pauses are often limited, because it takes confidence to *hold your ground* to allow your words to take up space and to remain silent without losing your concentration, yet crucial communication takes place in the time allowed by a pause. One piece of information should be digested before another is presented. There is often pressure to speak rapidly, to get it all said so that the class can get on with the work, when often what is being said is an absolutely essential part of the work. Pausing before important phrases, and before and after names and dates, can aid the listeners' memory retention of key facts.

Rhythm and energy

In order to deliver language effectively it is important to speak at a reasonable rate so that information can be processed. It is also worth pointing out that rate is the speed at which an individual word or group of words is spoken. Pace on the other hand can be thought of as the overall energy and rhythm of the delivery of an entire speech, so that you can speak individual words clearly and concisely, but keep the general pace driving forward energetically. This means you can have clarity, energy and precision as well as a sense of the rapidity of language flowing in rhythmic cadences. We believe the most effective way of gaining confidence in the ability to use words is to practise speaking words that have been carefully selected, that trigger exciting and interesting sound patterns and images. In other words, read aloud from the verse and prose that make up the wealth of our literature, the joy you will experience when you 'feel and taste' the vowels and consonants in the mouth is intensely rewarding. Speak passages that you feel passionately about; words that reflect your ideas and feelings. When the commitment is behind the word the voice does the work for you.

Vocal spontaneity

A more difficult aspect for the teacher to master is the ability to make old knowledge sound new. For most teachers the information they give the class has been known to them for a very long time. Some teachers may have taught the same course for many years, but the truly effective teacher is able to impart the information as though it was as new to her or him as to the class. When enthusiasm is natural, not pushed or forced and the speaker is using breath freely without any postural or tension problems, most of the aspects that determine the 'interesting' voice take care of themselves. Often, however, the speaker has developed a habit of sounding monotonous. This habit may have developed over a number of years and indeed may have been with the teacher as a child or an adolescent. Habits such as vocal monotony can develop during a period of insecurity or vulnerability and often, when the phase passes, the habit remains. For some adolescents the idea of standing up in class and reading or speaking in front of their peers is terrifying, the jaw tightens and all vocal variety is suppressed. For others a vocal quality is assumed as part of a survival strategy, such as the adolescent 'cool', 'street cred' approach which may involve a very limited use of range. Generally these phases are natural stages of development, but like posture the muscles often hold the pattern after the phase has passed.

Gesture

Gesture provides a natural reinforcement to what is being said. French and Italian speakers are perceived as using a lot of arm and hand movement to reinforce what they are saying, whereas this is less noticeable in English or German speakers. Obviously there are exceptions to every rule, but in general gesture has cultural implications and roots. This use of gesture is referred to as non-verbal communication and within this category the term 'body language' is frequently used to refer to all the means by which we communicate other than speech. These range from posture to small movements of the fingers, from eye contact to the way in which we shake hands. As with vocal variety, gesture should be the end result of thought processes and should stem from the desire to communicate those thoughts and ideas to the listener. Imposed gesture is quickly identified as artificial. Gesture works best when the speaker is sufficiently relaxed to integrate mind, voice and body in a total gestalt. Excessive gesture distracts from the very message you are trying to convey.

Presentation

All aspects of self-presentation contribute to this unspoken communication from how we are dressed to the way in which we cut our hair. Whether we like it or not, we are communicating all the time and people are continually making value judgements about us, which will determine the way in which they interact with us. Within the teaching profession, value judgements made of teachers by pupils will critically affect the relationship between teacher and pupil and influence, for better or worse, the dynamics within the classroom. The same is true among fellow professionals in whatever occupation, so the dynamics of the workplace are often affected for good or ill by something as simple as the clothes we wear, our posture, our voice quality and our national and regional accent.

Accent and dialect

Recognition should also be given to the fact that accent and dialect are often the criteria on which initial impressions are formed. Intrinsically they carry certain intonation patterns, e.g. a Welsh or Indian accent has a much more musical quality than, say, a German or Russian accent, but along with the musicality of the former comes a 'penalty clause', which is that these accents may be perceived as being much less authoritative. The habitual inflection pattern which gives the more musical sound can at times be falsely interpreted as questioning and uncertain.

Accent and the assumptions that are made about accents are well documented (John Honey 1989) and should, we believe, be challenged in the classroom, otherwise change will never occur. Nevertheless newly-qualified teachers with a specific regional accent, embarking on their first job in another part of the country, would do well to do so with the knowledge of how teenagers may react. Despite adolescent desires to be different the fact is that *being different* is something teenagers make strenuous efforts to avoid, from the clothes that they wear, to the films they watch, to the language that they use. A teacher with a different accent may be positively perceived or, conversely, the difference may be the basis for ridicule. Younger children seem often much more generous, but adolescents sometimes take their attitudes from the 'soaps' and these do nothing to break the stereotypical assumptions of regional accent, but rather reinforce them.

The accent with which you speak is usually the one spoken in the area in which you were raised and the one your primary carer used. Today, however, so many family units move from one area to another that many children have parents with different accents or even different mother tongues. Children who move from one area to another in their early years generally adopt the accent of their peer group in an effort to conform and to be accepted. This transition from one accent to another happens very quickly, in some children in the period of a few weeks.

Usually once you enter the middle teens your accent is less likely to alter; adults seldom significantly change their accents unless for very specific political or socio-cultural reasons. We know of one teacher from Leicester who has taught in South East London for twenty years. His accent is completely 'London'; he consciously allowed it to change because he felt it was easier for the class to relate to him. This is not a common occurrence but it does illustrate the considerable significance we place on accent. We are all 'vocal chameleons', most of us recognise that we have 'telephone voices' and that we slightly adapt our speech according to changing situations. We would, however, never suggest that any teacher should eradicate or seek to eradicate his or her accent; the richness of regional and national accents should enrich the life of the classroom. Nevertheless, people's accents are devalued. A Jamaican teacher who attended one of our courses was misusing her voice in an attempt to consciously alter her accent. After attending the course her written comment was as follows, '... felt valued as a Jamaican, I wasn't put down. Hurrah!' Whether this teacher had been 'put down' in the past because of her accent we do not know, but certainly she felt that a lack of respect for her nationality was inextricably linked to her accent and the perception other people had of it and hence of her.

What teachers should do, however, is to ensure clarity and vocal spontaneity, whatever their accent, and promote tolerance in children by encouraging them to talk about the diversity of speech in the school, community and region. When children understand the reason for differences they cease to mock them.

Paralinguistic features

So what other factors affect first impressions? The first five minutes are critical. We make value judgements about appearance, voice, clothes and posture and we then decide whether this person is someone that we think we will like or not like, who we can relate to or not relate to. Albert Mehrabian, a psychologist, suggested in 1972 that 55% of the impression we form of others is visual, i.e., we make decisions on what we see; the person's appearance, posture, body language, facial expression and eye contact, while only 38% of the impression we form of others is auditory, that is, what we hear, the voice quality, the pitch of the voice, the pace and use of pause, the clarity of speech and the accent that the person has. Only 7% of the impression we form of others is determined by the words that they say. What is said initially is very low on the list. It seems almost unbelievable that through what appears a rather arbitrary set of criteria we are making decisions that will affect our relationships for perhaps years to come, but that in fact is what happens. The validity of this form of judgement lies in the fact that most people, when asked how often they have altered their first impression of someone, will respond, 'rarely'. The number of times that we do alter our first impression of someone is so limited that we tend to remember when it occurs.

This judging process is a very normal process within us all, but as Rogers (1975) noted, a major barrier to interpersonal communication lies in our natural tendency to judge – to approve or disapprove of the statements of the other person. Statements do not need to be verbal; we make a statement about ourselves with, as has been said earlier, our clothes, our hair, our facial expression and our body language. So how does this process work? When we form an impression of other people, we are influenced by our own set of beliefs and values. When these values and beliefs are extreme, objective assessment becomes impossible, colour prejudice being a particularly evident and malicious example of this, as is sexual, gender and age prejudice. In forming relationships with other people we want to have our own ideas and beliefs reflected; we tend to like people 'like ourselves'. In part this is because we can understand and recognise these 'like-minded' people and in part because the differences we perceive in others can be very threatening. In the same way teachers undoubtedly need to recognise that pupils and parents, staff members and school visitors, will be making these instinctive judgements at the beginning of every school year and past pupils may reflect back their judgements of a particular teacher. 'You've got Mrs Bough this year. Oh goodness, she is so boring and it is really difficult to hear her.' Consequently the received wisdom is that Mrs Bough is boring and inaudible, even if this was a value judgement made by a pupil several years before.

It is also important to recognise that the tendency to evaluate is very much heightened in those situations where feelings and emotions are deeply involved. The stronger our feelings, the more likely it is that there will be no middle ground; there will be two ideas, two feelings, two judgements, all missing each other. For teachers this is often the situation; the pupils are anxious about moving into a new class, and the teacher is equally anxious about the new pupils; what will the class be like, will there be problems of discipline, will there be children with special needs? An incorrect assumption early on in a student–teacher relationship can determine the on-going communication, often with critical results. After all there are few professions where such an intimate relationship exists over such an extended period as that between teachers and their pupils.

Given the need to maximise the opportunity to communicate effectively, how can this be achieved? There are several well-recognised communication facilitators which can be applied in any situation.

Facilitating communication

Positioning

How we position ourselves in relation to the other person or persons is very important and each position 'says' something. We cannot always choose where to sit, but the position in which we sit can affect the interaction which takes place in significant and predictable ways. We tend to sit opposite someone we are competing against; this obviously has something to do with the fact that we like to be able to monitor their movements. In teaching there is very little choice, positioning is fairly well prescribed by the number of pupils and the need to view the blackboard, overheads, or audio-visual aids. In primary school this is easier; more teaching can be undertaken in a round-table setting which also encourages a more participative atmosphere, if a more noisy one. Wherever possible teachers should try to vary the placement of desks and try to encourage more participative positions. When we think of interview situations, for example when visiting the doctor, or someone in authority, this 'opposite position' appears to be the preferred position, although more doctors are introducing a diagonal position *vis-à-vis* the patient, which is similar to that of an 'interview' situation. Alongside another individual is the recognised co-operative position, but that is more rarely seen in formal situations. Needless to say this would be most difficult for teachers to achieve in junior or secondary schools, but it could be achieved in small group tutorials or discussion groups and is certainly to be recommended.

Distance

Distance from another person or a group of people would not at first sight appear to be an important aspect of communication, but it has been recognised as having a considerable effect. Studies have highlighted appropriate distances for specific communication situations. From nought to one-and-a-half feet is an appropriate distance for intimate social situations, one foot to four feet for personal situations, talking to good friends or colleagues, while social/consultative situations require a distance of four to ten feet to be maintained between people. For public situations more than ten feet between speaker and audience is appropriate. This suggests that for most teachers there is a positioning mix within the classroom environment. For those pupils sitting at the front of the class they and the teacher relate at a 'personal' distance, while for those further back they and the teacher relate at a 'social/consultative position' distance. The result of this is a mis-match within the dynamics of the class as far as positioning is concerned. Teachers should be aware of this and attempt to compensate for it by perhaps addressing more comments to the back of the class, spending more time making eye contact with those at the back of the class, and looking at their posture in relationship to those at the back and indeed deliberately moving around the class.

Body language

One of the interesting things to have been discovered is how individuals who are in tune mentally or who respect the other person, tend to mirror each other's posture and this is a significant clue when looking at group dynamics. Those who are in tune are usually looking towards each other and reflecting back each other's posture, while those who are not compatible show definite signs of defensive body posture, arms crossed, leaning away and lack of eye contact. It is perhaps appropriate for teachers to reflect on some of the current studies available on body language which may offer strategies for them in terms of classroom management, so that they observe aspects of body language which may signal disinterest, anger or depression.

Explaining

Teachers often feel that they have to spend a great deal of class time in explaining and re-explaining information. Given that most teachers talk for two-thirds of the time in classrooms (Flanders 1970), and two-thirds of their talk is lecturing, then explaining is clearly a common activity in the classroom. Estimates of the proportion of time spent on explaining by teachers vary from 10% to 30% (Dunkin and Biddle 1974). Often this time is both vocally tiring and frustrating and can be unprofitable. If the quality of the explanation is poor, then the time is spent ineffectually. A review of the literature suggests that good explanations are not only clearly structured, they are also interesting. There has been considerable work in this field in the past 14 years (Brown and Hatton 1982; Brown and Armstrong 1984). Interestingly, pupils' views on explaining appear to have been consistent over a period of at least fifty years as Hart (1934) found that the principal reasons for liking a teacher were based on the teacher's helpfulness in terms of school work and their ability to explain lessons clearly.

Explanation: strategies and skills

Explaining can be described as a mixture of strategies and skills which need to be mastered if explanations are going to be effective.

Teachers and indeed anyone who is in the explanation business need to remember that. Some of the strategies cited by Brown (1986) are that:

- topics should be analysed into main parts;
- links should be established between these parts;
- the characteristics of the learner must be accounted for when adapting plans;
- if there are any rules involved in the explanation they should be defined.

Brown also suggests that those giving the explanation must have certain basic skills, skills such as:

- clarity and fluency;
- emphasis and interest;
- using examples;
- organisation and feedback.

Clarity and fluency can be achieved through defining new terms, through use of explicit language and through avoiding vagueness. Emphasis and interest can be achieved by variations in gesture, by use of media and materials, by use of voice and pauses, by repetition, paraphrasing or verbal cueing. When using examples they should be clear, appropriate and concrete in sufficient quantity and where applicable, positive and negative. The organisation of the lecture, lesson or explanation should be in a logical and clear sequence with the use of link words and phrases. Feedback to the listener should provide opportunities for questions, there should be an assessment of what the listener has understood of the main idea and additionally the individual giving the explanation should seek to understand the attitudes and values of those to whom he or she is speaking.

In studies reported by Schonell, Roe and Middleton (1962) and Brown (1979, 1980) students cited their main dissatisfaction with teachers and lecturers to be: failure to emphasise main points, failure to pitch at an appropriate level, inaudibility, incoherence and reading aloud from notes.

Many of the above issues which cause student dissatisfaction are easy to remedy and could make a considerable difference to class response. It is worth remembering that good communication skills not only indicate that you have respect for your audience, but also that you value yourself.

Oral skills

For many people the thought of standing up and addressing a group rates as their greatest fear. The young people who are now pupils in schools will be facing the same fears in adult life and it is sensible educational practice to develop their skills and confidence in the area of interpersonal communication skills. If young people are given the opportunity to gain the experience and confidence needed for easy, structured and sustained public speaking, those fears need never materialise and the adults of tomorrow will be much more effective speakers.

Too often the crowded curriculum does not allow for work of this kind, other than a token amount in the English syllabus. Traditionally in the United Kingdom the public schools have placed great emphasis on oral skills but all children should be offered the same opportunity. Practice in oratory can be gained by reading aloud public speeches by the great orators as they teach a lot about effective structures. Debating societies, drama groups and involvement in reading and addressing assemblies all offer an opportunity to gain these skills. Business and industrial courses are currently teaching simple formulae for effective speech. While they are a wonderful starting point, they are easily identified and the devices of manipulation are often obvious. Max Atkinson's (1984) study of oratory and politics makes fascinating reading for anyone wanting to improve the structure of formal speeches. The information it offers is undoubtedly useful for teachers.

Chapter 7
Words in the
Classroom

Words Words Words

Vocalisation without language has little meaning. In the classroom, communication between teacher and student is usually word based. Many of the teachers we meet feel that their vocal problems arise from the profound difficulty they have with finding and using words effectively. Voices tend to work best when what is being said is important to the speaker and subsequently stimulating to the listener. Teachers are often conscious that their difficulties began as a result of a lack of focus on oral skills in their own education and feel that they would like to offer a richer language environment to their students. It would seem appropriate therefore to use this chapter to offer suggestions for raising the verbal profile of the classroom.

The teacher uses words, either spoken or written, in almost every activity he or she undertakes. Language and its delivery underpin the way knowledge is imparted. The modern approach to the process of education is a two-way exchange of ideas between teacher and student and therefore depends upon the ability of both parties to participate effectively. Our society is moving towards a use of technology that does not encourage verbally interactive skills. Today's children are used to interacting with computer technology and obtain both entertainment and information from screens. While the ability for children to use technology is essential, it is imperative that the balance is redressed by the equivalent development of interesting and useful speech and language skills.

The Effects of Technology

With the need to economise, many schools, colleges and universities are becoming more dependent on technology as a method of teaching.

It is seen as a way of releasing teachers from contact time and often provides an effective method of instruction for subjects such as (ironically) languages. As a society we are becoming more and more media influenced resulting in a reduced range of language being used by young schoolchildren, many of whom spend an inordinate amount of time as passive *viewers* rather than active *doers* and while the educational value of television cannot be underestimated, reduced reading time has led to an erosion of the broad range of expression available to children. It is not surprising, therefore, that many teachers feel that their students use language mechanically and automatically, that they use words without thought.

Many teachers express a keen interest in returning to the teaching of oral skills, skills that provide society with the opportunity to enjoy words and foster a delight in the speaking of well-ordered and expressive language, skills which have been 'sidelined' by the crowded curriculum. It is important to be clear that the move is not to re-instate the old-fashioned, class-based 'elocution' classes of the early part of the century. These can be divisive and may restrict language rather than free it. What many teachers want is to encourage a move towards ensuring that children of all cultural backgrounds are not disenfranchised because they are not given the language skills which allow them to express their needs clearly and achieve their goals. There are several organisations who have worked tirelessly over a number of years to promote such work. The English Speaking Board founded by Christabel Burniston has done much to stimulate an interest in spoken language. It offers exams in oral communication for schools, colleges, commerce and industry. Public speaking festivals and competitions organised by the English Speaking Union have also contributed to the development of the 'oracy' of the young people who are fortunate enough to attend a school that participates. There are also many local festivals which promote the speaking of verse, prose and reading as a performance skill and even broadcasting. In many schools teachers of English take responsibility for productions and festivals within the school, but with the loss of the specialist the time-consuming task means extra unpaid work for the generous volunteer.

Spoken English in the Curriculum

Undoubtedly the more discursive approach to spoken language allows teacher–student relationships to become proficient in informal conversational practice but it is critical to recognise the power of the formal structures that underpin oratory. The National Curriculum in Britain now has an element of spoken English in the General Certificate of Secondary Education syllabi but this is not enormously challenging or demanding for many verbally able students. The inclusion of English literature as well as English language as a compulsory subject has been welcomed by all. However, it is not only the pupils who need consideration and help with the delivery of language but also the teachers, who in many instances feel they too would benefit from help both with their own skills and with devising ways of stimulating discussion and verbal analysis.

Ideas from Outside

Apart from the excellent published material available there are currently many opportunities for staff and students to receive an injection of new ideas and stimuli from outside organisations. Some theatre companies run workshops on the plays they produce and offer follow-up packs with suggestions for both written and oral exercises. In the United Kingdom The Royal Shakespeare Company has an Education Department which not only gives workshops for students on the current season and sets up residencies in schools, but also runs an annual Shakespeare School, which is designed to meet the needs of teachers teaching Shakespeare at GCSE and A level, which brings together the three overlapping worlds of theatre practice, contemporary Shakespeare scholarship and educational practice.

Making Words Physical

Young people are often discouraged when faced with language which to them seems alienating. By entering into language physically; and by speaking words out loud and putting their analytical skills aside for a time, a fuller more meaningful understanding is achieved. Helpful exercises in this approach can be found in *The Actor and the Text* by Cicely Berry (1993), who began working with teachers and young people over twenty years ago. Through her need to find ways of making the language of the classics accessible to the young, she has made a seminal contribution to the teaching of language in schools and formulated an approach which involves the whole class actively entering into the language physically and vocally.

The experience of speaking the texts is all too often overlooked in the classroom situation, where the good readers are generally the only ones who get the opportunity. The Globe Theatre in London has an Education Department doing text related work, as does the Royal National Theatre and many regional and fringe theatres. Theatres in other countries run similar outreach projects. Although the work they offer may not specifically focus on speech, the work is all practical and drama based and will encourage debate in addition to helping the teacher with less experience of drama to explore unconventional approaches to text and language teaching.

Finding Help

We have met teachers who feel intimidated by having to read verse, prose and dramatic texts aloud. There are classes held through Adult Education Courses which may be useful, such as a drama group or a public-speaking class. Toast-masters and other similar societies offer opportunities to develop skills in formal speaking. Popular at present are groups which offer the opportunity to explore storytelling, oral history and reminiscence, which are all skills useful to the teacher, and can be used to enrich the oral tradition within the class. Some people prefer individual classes and in the United Kingdom, The Society of Teachers of Speech and Drama provides a list of recognised teachers, and similar societies exist in other countries. There are often workshop advertisements in theatrical and professional journals, which are available at larger libraries.

In-service Training Days

When a group of teachers from one school identify the need for help in a particular area, it is usual to approach the school administration and request sponsorship from the Staff Development Fund or arrange an in-service training day. Maths and science teachers may have finished with English lessons after GCSE and certainly some of them feel their facility with words would be supported by workshops in the use of language. For the infant and primary teacher illuminating learning through speech as the 'story-teller' is enormously useful in developing a 'way with words', and there are those teachers who have come to the profession because of a natural instinctive skill in communication and even performance. In many institutions the skills of the advanced level and technical teacher are closer to those of the university lecturer than those of the classroom teacher and they find themselves delivering long tracts of memorised material. In these cases the style of teaching is closer to public speaking. The art of the public speaker is needed in these instances and is explored in

Chapter 9. This art can be enhanced by developing an interest in debating and there are teachers who have learned to deliver speeches effectively through the experience of having to run a debating society or by entering groups of students into public-speaking competitions. Many who take on this responsibility complain that they are not being given the training they need for what is an essential part of their job. Where only a few teachers from a school require a specific workshop it is sometimes possible to approach the local Teachers Centre who could provide training.

Special Language Needs

In the infant school the acquisition of language is rapid and the child explores words and masters syntax through books, stories and play which become a significant way of making sense of their world. The classroom is an ideal setting for the development of the pupil's ability to use language. It is the place where early signs of special needs can be recognised. It is often the child's parents who overlook the early signs of problems in language development, sometimes because the child is their first and they have no comparison to make between children, and sometimes, as in the case of delayed or inaccurate speech sounds, parents do not notice problems such as 'lisps' or difficulty with consonant combinations simply because they are not in the position to be objective.

More and more children now attend playgroups and nursery schools and here language and speech delay is fairly closely monitored as playgroup and nursery school leaders are increasingly aware of the problems that can occur. Fortunately there is ever more awareness of the work of the speech and language therapist and the intervention that is available, yet there are still a number of children who are overlooked. Indeed there are instances where children have specific phonological problems that parents will not accept as needing treatment or that they perceive as being rather appealing, such as inter-dental 'lisps' or /w/ for /r/ substitution. The problem for the primary school teacher is that if the child is unable to perceive the difference between one sound and another in speech, then it is even more difficult for them to perceive the difference between one sound and the other when reading, and of course an appreciation of phonics is an essential pre-reading skill. In the same way, subtle difficulties with language either on the expressive or receptive side can be overlooked and only come to light at school entry when there is more need for the child to use language to express more abstract thoughts and ideas. Issues of receptive language difficulty such as semantic relationships, word classes, oral directions, or expressive language such as recalling sentences, formulating sentences or sentence assembly, can have been overlooked and only become apparent when having to use language in a more precise form. Children learn some of their early speech skills from repeating what they hear, and from nursery rhymes and songs, which because of their rhythm, rhyme, harmony and disharmony of different combinations of vowels and consonants, are easily committed to memory and these verses remain with them for the rest of their lives.

With the increasing voluntary assistance given in the early stages of reading practice, teachers should alert the volunteers to the early warning signals of speech and/or language delay. It is often these 'helpers' who have the most one-to-one contact with the child. The Royal College of Speech and Language Therapists offers advice in recognising speech and language problems and may be contacted to locate the local clinic or specialist centre.

Language Opportunities in the Secondary School

Many of the teachers we met were particularly keen to explore ways of opening up debates with adolescents. Adolescence is a time when alternative views are normal and it is important that schools recognise this and allow ideas to be expressed through debate and discussion. Speaking the words of others is often the first step to being able to find words for oneself. English literature offers such an enormous variety of wonderfully honed and precisely constructed examples of the expression of every conceivable emotion. When offered to young people for exploration and consideration such verse or prose often releases the words within the individual and allows their own thoughts to be manifested in language. The more interactive and vocal the English class becomes, the better. Teaching students to appreciate and 'own' literature can only be wholly successful when they experience the speaking of it. Many adolescents have needs which they are not able to express or deal with adequately, such as feelings of rage and grief, huge enthusiasms and devotion to particular groups or individuals. If teachers can help students to express their needs and help them to find the words with which to make some sense of their lives, then true education takes place.

We have mentioned some of the opportunities for the use of verse and prose with adolescents. Both can be used with all age groups from the playgroup upward. All too often, verse is only used by the English teachers and in drama, but the opportunity to use poetry in history and social studies, and in fact in almost every class in the school, is often sadly neglected.

Choral Speaking

Choral verse was a popular way of teaching children verse up until the 1970s. It has lost popularity because it was seen as being taught for all the wrong reasons. At one stage it was used as a way of imposing 'received pronunciation' on children who had regional accents, and therefore discarded. There are, however, many positive reasons for encouraging classes to speak together, the most important of all being simply that it offers many children, who are not exposed to verse the opportunity to come in contact with it and to be exposed to the physical joy of the experience. There is always a danger that the teacher will feel the need to make the children sound 'correct' rather than allowing them to feel the energy and the sound of the language, the sheer enjoyment of telling the story, and communicating the material to the audience. The demands made by the exercise go far beyond the simple act of memorising words. The speaking of well-selected verse demands the development of a feeling for rhythm that informs the child's own speech and writing and their appreciation of rhythm in verse and prose. It also offers the valuable experience of speaking language rather than analysing it. This adds a physical and organic dimension to work with words at any stage. A group can also explore verse by taking a line each around the classroom, responding to the vocal energy of the words and of each other, and developing a communal voice. Working towards sharing of work with other classes and parents can be an enriching experience for all but it is sometimes a mistake to concentrate on the performance of group verse rather than simply speaking it for its own sake. The process should always be more important than the product. Speaking words that are carefully chosen to be part of a well-shaped and honed structure and are part of an overall intention to be communicated, take the words beyond the page and 'into the mouth', so that the pupils know what it feels like to speak them and not just to read them. The speaking of powerful words leads to the empowerment of individuals and the understanding that the words that are presented on the page have enormous power and influence to change people, situations and ultimately lives. The person who can express him or herself in words feels in command not only of language, but also of his or her life. The frustration that often leads to violence can, instead of turning in on itself, be channelled through language to become both a positive creative force and to lead to a better understanding of self and others. Cicely Berry (1992) says, 'For when you cannot speak, what is there left but violence?' There are many psychologists, welfare workers and teachers who would agree with this but in the need to equip young people with writing skills the spoken word often gets neglected. The need to develop the oral skills of our society is obvious but who takes on the burden of the additional teaching?

The Loss of the Specialist

A common complaint among teachers is that with the loss of the specialist positions of the speech and drama and music teacher, many teachers find themselves doing a job they do not feel qualified to undertake. They feel that they look like charlatans, having to patch together classes that they are then under-confident in teaching. A significant number of teachers end up teaching subjects in which they did not originally specialise. Some teachers feel a pressure to accept additional duties and are fearful of admitting they are not able to teach either speech-based work or singing. The demands are increasing, and the school should offer the proper training by means of in-service courses for anyone in this position. A teacher we met found herself teaching singing because she was the only member of staff in her village school who played the piano. 'The worst aspect of teaching singing was that I was so embarrassed at having to demonstrate. Eventually, after becoming extremely anxious about it and on occasions feeling that my throat completely closed up, I went to a wonderful singing teacher at my own expense and gained some confidence. I now enjoy it.'

Singing

While most singing teachers do a wonderful job in the musical life of the school, some singing teachers of the past have much to answer for where children have been adversely affected and in some cases scarred by thoughtless and often ignorant remarks. In our workshops, teachers (often and probably not co-incidentally, those experiencing vocal problems) recalled humiliating remarks made by class or singing teachers about their supposed 'inability' to sing. Typically it has been suggested to the child that they should not sing, but rather 'mouth' the words. Such remarks are never child-centred but are usually concerned with the teacher's, or the head teacher's, desire to produce a 'polished' performance for an adult audience. No one ever suggests that the child who finds maths difficult should simply refrain from the exercise. Why, then, is it acceptable to stop some children from singing when what they need to improve their pitching is more practise at it, not less. With enough practise and positive encouragement, the child who pitches normally in speech can be given the confidence to pitch accurately in song. Singing should be a natural, joyous and fundamental part of every child's education and like choral verse the process should be more important than the product.

The teaching of singing to young children, who in many cases have hearing that is not yet sufficiently sophisticated to pitch accurately, should also involve teaching them to listen through a series of auditory training exercises. These lessons in listening will have a positive effect in many other areas of school life. Singing can also provide excellent practice in speech sounds as definition is required and produced when the children are committed to the act of singing.

The singing lesson, like the choral speaking lesson, offers a wonderful opportunity to establish the essential basics of easy, free spontaneous voice use. Children can be encouraged to align themselves well and stand with the weight on both feet and with a long spine. They can to taught to breath 'down' rather than to take a 'big breath', to release the shoulders, relax the jaw and to keep the head balanced on the top of the spine. The opportunity to establish these fundamentals should not be lost and better still is the chance to provide the experience of being part of a group that is involved in the creating of communal sound. Much has been written about the act of singing and the loss of this essentially primal social activity from our culture. It is also important, as with verse, to select material that not only reflects the majority school population but also extends an understanding of the minority cultures within the school.

Music and verse can greatly enhance empathy with cultures and with countries and periods, in history and geography classes. It can naturally be a useful way of extending work on other languages. The singing of traditional songs allows children to enter into the narrative tradition and to develop an interest in story telling which is often lacking in the modern family unit.

Children with Particular Needs

Children with stammers sometimes find a great freedom in song as the process of singing, particularly in a group, allows them to enjoy the experience of communication without the stress that many of them find in speaking by themselves. Many adult stammerers will report that they rarely, if ever, stammer when singing, in the same way that many find talking to animals and small children a relatively stammer-free experience. Within the classroom teachers are often uncertain how to approach the stammerer in order not to marginalise them from speaking situations, but at the same time not to force them to speak in situations which they find difficult. It is important to try to establish with the speech and language therapist the best approach for each child.

In classes where there are a number of children with special needs, it is undoubtedly difficult to formulate individual learning programmes but certainly many children with special needs will enjoy the rhythm and participative nature of song. There is a significant body of knowledge now available through the work of music therapists which will offer a way into language through music for children with special needs.

The value of singing goes beyond the technical aspects of breath, pitch, communication and precision of sounds, because as with all language, its delivery is a gestalt, involving body, breath, mind, intention, rhythm, musicality and interpretation. It not only develops musicality but also the interpersonal and ensemble skills of group timing, anticipation and co-operation. For many children the act of group speaking or singing allows them a great deal of freedom to explore their own creative powers and imagination.

Chapter 8
Vocal Health

Strategies to Maintain Effective Voice

One of the perennial topics that is raised during teacher workshop discussions is how teachers can most effectively limit vocal strain within their working environment and how best they can preserve their voices against the demands of the classroom.

The historical perspective

The lack of emphasis placed on the vocal needs and professional demands of teachers has been unashamedly highlighted throughout this book but it is hoped that this will soon change and certainly the test case in 1994, where a head teacher (forced to retire early after her voice was reduced to a whisper by the demands of teaching) won a claim for industrial injury benefit, was a landmark. Ruling in the case, a social security tribunal accepted that the teacher had damaged her voice through having to raise it in order to be heard over the noise level in the school's open plan classroom. While there is no guarantee that voice training would have prevented her from losing her voice, there is substantial evidence that voice training to meet the demands of teaching would have been able to mitigate against the worst effects of the profession (Martin 1994). It is also clear that significant early warning vocal signals are often ignored by teachers who assume that these signals 'come with the territory', so to speak.

Early warning signals

So what can be done to prevent potential vocal difficulties and what are some of the early warning signs that teachers should be aware

of? A worrying concern is the lack of attention that these early warning signs of vocal abuse and misuse receive. This is due largely to the
lack of vocal health information and education that is available to
teachers but, in addition, in every staffroom there are teachers who
are experiencing similar difficulties and so this is seen as normal and
not demanding of particular attention. The unspoken message
therefore is that this is a problem we all expect to have at some time
or another; it will probably improve so don't worry about it. In view
of the current funding difficulties, teachers are very reluctant to take
time off work, with what could be perceived as a fairly minor
ailment. This is a familiar situation in many schools and underlines
the commitment of the majority of teachers, who endeavour to 'keep
going', irrespective of the state of their voice.

According to Jackson (1968) teachers engage in 200–300
exchanges every hour of their working day, which is an amazing
1200–1800 exchanges during their working day and does not take
into account any exchanges during the lunch hour or at meetings
after school. A recent study in Japan (Matsuda *et al.*,1993) is of interest. An analysis of speaking behaviour was made among vocal abuse
patients. When the speaking habits of teachers and patients from
other professions who had vocal fold nodules were looked at, they
discovered that these two groups spoke three times longer than, for
example, vocally healthy office workers. The teachers and patients
had a long phonation time (102 minutes over an 8-hour period) and
half the total phonation time was at high intensity, i.e. at 80dB and
over. The study showed that after-school phonation time was very
short, so if the results of this small study are extended it is probably
quite safe to assume that for most teachers the same speech pattern
will apply – extensive speaking periods at high intensity during
school hours with much less voicing out of school.

Repertoire of strategies

There is undoubtedly a need for teachers to formulate a repertoire of
classroom strategies which can be used to overcome or at least alleviate some of the difficulties inherent in classroom practice. This chapter offers ideas and suggestions which may be adapted for each
individual's requirements. It is recommended that teachers and
lecturers collaborate with colleagues in building up a library of
suggestions suitable for their particular workplace and which can be
accessed by all staff. Perhaps this information could be kept in the
staffroom and displayed prominently so that staff focus on the issues.

As so many issues of health and safety are currently being addressed in education, voice care for teachers should be taken much more seriously.

Postural Implications

In addition to the fundamentals discussed in Chapter 5 it is important to monitor specific classroom postures which can become habitual and lead to chronic physical and vocal problems. The most obvious problem arises from the height of the desks in the infant school which require the teacher to spend sustained periods of time leaning over while speaking to children or marking their work. There is also a tendency for many people who have spent significant amounts of time in study to be unaware of poor head and neck alignment and this may lead ultimately to what is often referred to as a 'Dowager's hump'. This is where there is a loss of alignment between head and neck and as a result the curvature of the spine at the level of the cervical cartilages becomes pronounced and can frequently be seen within the older population. As a result of this, the head–neck–spine relationship is altered and the position of the larynx within the pharynx is changed; sometimes constriction of the larynx can occur and changes result in the configuration of the pharynx and the vocal tract which can result in a rather 'squeezed' pharyngeal sound. If possible the teacher should crouch beside pupils, or draw up a chair alongside the child when explaining or helping with work.

It is also important that the individual teacher tries to monitor his or her posture when working at his or her desk or when giving instructions to the class. Keep the weight well distributed across both feet with knee joints flexible and unlocked. Try to avoid standing with arms crossed, as breathing is restricted and the body tends to slump forward. Ideally the pelvis should be level, with space between the hips and lower ribs. The spine should be long and the shoulders low with the neck free and the head well balanced on the top of the spine. Throughout the day it is advisable to check the alignment of the body and be aware of neck and facial tension and any building up of tension in the jaw.

Early Indications of Vocal Misuse and Abuse

For many teachers the first indication that they are abusing or misusing their voice comes, not as a specific voice production problem, but rather as a feeling of tightness and tension in the neck. Teachers report that they are aware of their throat feeling rather stiff and indeed some report a feeling of generalised soreness while others report that at times they have feelings of considerable pain. As a general rule teachers tend to ignore these symptoms, putting them down to tension or stress, but they can be early indications of undue effort being put into producing voice. In Chapter 4 the link between respiration, relaxation and voice was discussed and the need to view each component as part of the whole was stressed. When voicing is effortful one of the major reasons is undue tension within the neck and shoulder area and this can be related firstly to posture and secondly to the individual teacher's lack of awareness of habitual posture and muscle state. Half spectacles which are often prescribed for those individuals who only need them for reading tend to encourage people to look up and over to see what is happening within the classroom, and this 'up and over' posture alters the neck, head and shoulder configuration. When working on the upper body teachers often will say that they had no idea that their shoulder position was habitually so high; it is only when one works on relaxing this area that this becomes so apparent. Indeed many report that this shoulder position never alters, whether driving, reading, walking or sitting.

It is worthwhile to take time during the working day to think about shoulder position. Can you lower them? Are they relaxed? Do you feel there is very little space between the base of your skull and your shoulders? By raising the shoulders we effectively limit the space within the pharynx and constrict the larynx, so voice is produced much less easily. In Chapter 10 we give suggestions for a range of exercises which can be done and several of the exercises will help with postural change. If you drive to work through busy traffic you might find that the tension experienced en route is established for the rest of your working day, so try and use the time to counteract the build-up of tension by lifting and releasing your neck and shoulders when an opportunity arises, at traffic lights for example or in the ever-increasing traffic tailbacks. Good driving posture should include support to the lower spine, not impose tension on the shoulder girdle, and maintain a released head and neck position.

Apart from the postural implications in terms of stress and tension sites, a rounded posture has an effect on communicative intent, as it portrays someone who appears to be lacking in authority and is much less effective in non-verbal communication terms than the individual who has an easy upright posture which quite effectively gives more weight to what is being said.

Once highlighted, this problem is not difficult to deal with but it does take time and awareness. Much can be done by individual monitoring of body posture, distinguishing between what is normal and what has become habitual. For some people achieving the 'new' posture is initially easy but difficult to maintain. Considerable effort has to be expended to make the 'new' seem comfortable and until it becomes established, far from seeming better, it may seem rather worse.

Teachers are often caricatured as individuals clad in academic gowns and weighed down by piles of books. Undoubtedly most teachers carry far too many books awkwardly with the weight slung across one shoulder. The best way to carry heavy weights is close to the body, cradled against the chest, or if you have to carry lots of books, divide them into two piles and make sure weight is well distributed, otherwise there can be undue strain on the spine and lower back (see Figure 10).

Figure 10: *Incorrect carrying position*

Sitting

Remember that the 'sitting' bones or ischium bones serve the same function as the feet and therefore when sitting try and get yourself well balanced and use these bones to support yourself adequately. It is important that if you are sitting for long periods of time, attention should be paid to the seating provided. Very often the seating in schools is not comfortable and it is important to remember that uncomfortable seating not only puts strain on our backs but also pressure on our abdomen. When slumping forward our breathing is restricted, when slumping backwards pressure is put on the lower spine, so if necessary bring in your own chair, one that offers adequate support to your back and is at a good level for working at your desk. As a guide to height Macdonald (1994) suggests you should be able to comfortably reach the surface of the desk; when your hands are flat on the surface your arms should be bent at a right-angle. Funding for a suitable chair may be available from the school; try and establish this first as often in special cases provision is made for teachers with 'special needs' to enable them to keep on teaching for as long as possible. When writing at your desk, table, or on your keyboard Macdonald suggests that one of the first requirements is to use a sloped surface, this creates far less strain on the wrists and is very simple to achieve by using a piece of board, or a tray with a support behind it, to make a sloped surface, similarly with a computer, angle the keyboard by using a support behind it. This might be a useful project for a design and technology class as it would not only teach the skills of technology but would introduce the principles of ergonomics.

When using the desk try not to use it to lean against during teaching periods, as the tendency when leaning against a desk is to do so with one buttock on the desk and one leg supporting the weight, thus throwing the body out of alignment.

Classrooms are notorious for the amount of material that needs to be kept 'available' for projects and teachers often have to move boxes of stationery, equipment, and project material from place to place, and as with carrying heavy weights, the potential for damaging the lower back is high. In the same way clearing out deep cupboards and high shelves can be difficult for teachers. Teachers with chronic shoulder pain or tension should invest in themselves, in terms of treatment. When the problem is chronic rather than acute, a series of massage sessions by a properly qualified practitioner can do much to improve the situation and prevent the 'knock on' effect of vocal problems which can result from poor posture. There is an instinctive protection response when muscles are damaged in some way, and as has been said, within the classroom problems in the neck, upper back or shoulder area can easily occur. Although not immediately apparent, heel height is also important; too high a heel can have the effect of tilting the body forward and so altering alignment, resulting in compensatory movement and tension in the lower back, neck and head. A low heel is generally preferable to no heel at all but each individual should wear shoes that are practical and comfortable.

Self-monitoring

A second reason for tension and effortful voicing is the difficulty some teachers have in monitoring the voice appropriately. Without training it is very difficult to accurately assess voice volume levels. The instinctive response when trying to make oneself heard is to increase volume and indeed at times shout 'over' noise. In that way we increase the effort we put into producing the sound and endeavour to 'push out' the voice. Teachers will often report that this is how they try to take control when a class is making a lot of noise. For untrained voice users this is not only hugely tiring but it is also counterproductive.

Individuals can be trained to shout easily and without straining the vocal folds, but being trained to shout is not necessary for most people, instead what is important is to acquire skills in alternative ways that vocally or non-vocally 'cut through' the noise. This may require a pitch that is higher or lower than the ambient noise. For the female teacher the use of an instrument such as a cymbal or tambourine may help to limit the strain on the voice. The male voice being generally lower in pitch and having more base resonance is sufficiently different from the high-pitched voices of children to be much more easily audible.

It should be possible to organise the class without shouting but this approach needs to be established from the very first meeting as it is virtually impossible to break the habit of inattention once it has become the norm. Ground rules should be set in place which allow for specific noisy times as well as quiet times but these must be negotiated with the class. In an ideal situation shouting should not be necessary but even the most resourceful teacher resorts to this very human reaction on occasions.

Much of the shouting that occurs in school is very damaging to the voice and indeed very tiring. It is also quite difficult for pupils, many of whom find constant shouting by the teacher both distracting and at times distressing. For the teacher concerned, the amount of vocal effort that they are making manifests itself in pain and tension in the neck and occasionally in the jaw and tongue. If you have no idea of how this feels those who are inexperienced or reluctant singers may remember the effort involved in maintaining the note when singing and the feeling of tightness in the neck and particularly under the jaw that can result. This feeling of tightness is the result of tension in the large tongue muscles which form a 'strap' under the chin. The point of insertion of these muscles is the hyoid bone, which as we have already seen has an intimate relationship with the positioning of the larynx within the throat and indeed changes in this positioning will affect the movement of the vocal folds. For many teachers this feeling of tension is one which they experience every day, luckily for some this tension does not create permanent vocal problems, but for many, the effort required is quite exhausting and using their voice is very difficult.

Loss of Range

Many teachers report that they no longer have the singing range that they used to have nor indeed can they make themselves heard over the normal classroom noise. While these teachers may have never experienced partial or complete voice loss, they have experienced a significant diminution of their vocal range and vocal effectiveness. One of the difficulties of this type of chronic vocal abuse and misuse lies in the fact that for many teachers the problem has been a slow but insidious one, indeed it is only when teachers are asked to think back to their vocal function when they started teaching and compare it to their present ability that they realise how much their range has diminished. Had the reduction in voice been sudden or complete then more attention might have been given to the problem and the teacher could have retained much more vocal flexibility.

Personal Strategies

There is much that can be done through the use of simple strategies. We have divided the following strategies into sections which we hope will make accessing the information a little easier.

Ventilation

There are a number of common causes of vocal abuse and misuse and several have their origins in environmental conditions which are endemic to school life. While some conditions are endemic it does not mean that there is no way to mitigate against them and certainly it is important to follow certain rules of vocal hygiene and voice care in order to prevent further abuse and misuse. Avoidance of laryngeal irritants is an important factor in vocal hygiene. The laryngeal mucosa is extremely sensitive so, in so far as it is possible, avoid smoky, dusty atmospheres. Teachers often work in buildings where ventilation is a problem, often because the windows are hermetically sealed and cannot be opened even partially. During the winter, when the central heating is turned on, classrooms can become too hot, and a very dry atmosphere will affect the respiratory tract and in turn the larynx. Air conditioning can have the same effect, so it is very important to be aware of the possible effects on the voice and to take steps to lessen the problems.

Liquid intake

Every teacher should ensure that they drink more than the national average! It is important to drink at least 1 litre of water, bottled or tap, sparkling or still, per day, in addition to that contained in the normal intake of liquid through drinks such as tea and coffee. Tea and coffee have a diuretic effect and as such can be dehydrating, so it is important to 'top up' with water in order to maintain the moisture level within the body at an optimum level. Indeed some specialists would suggest avoiding tea and coffee completely and substituting herbal teas. The maxim 'pee pale' is a good rule to follow; urine that is pale in colour indicates a good level of hydration in the body. (For those on medication it is useful to remember that vitamin B makes urine darker in colour.) While the vocal folds cannot be directly lubricated by drinking, an increased fluid intake will increase our general body fluid level and prevent dehydration, which is particularly important when the vocal folds are in any way vulnerable.

It is particularly important to keep the fluid level topped up in women of menopausal age, where as we have seen the vocal folds are subject to tissue change, as well as in those individuals who are heavy smokers or drinkers. While we are aware of the problems of keeping water in the classroom (certain schools have a rule preventing teachers drinking while teaching), it is most important for teachers to endeavour to keep water at hand, if at all possible. One solution is to introduce a humidifier into the classroom to limit atmospheric dryness or if all else fails, bring in a goldfish in a bowl!

Teachers who are working on the Information and Design Technology syllabus should try and remember that if working on materials with lathes or saws which are likely to create dust, they should wear a mask as small dust particles are very irritating to the vulnerable larynx. In the same way working with paints or varnishes can be irritating. Teachers who are taking swimming classes in heavily chlorinated swimming pools should be vigilant in case of possible adverse reactions.

Steaming

This is a very effective way to introduce moisture into the vocal tract and minimise some of the dryness that one experiences with colds, vocal fatigue and stress. Either use the tried and tested method of a steaming bowl of water, used with a towel draped over the head (it is not necessary to add herbal extracts to the water) or alternatively have a long shower remembering to inhale the steam, preferably through both the nose and mouth. This can be useful in the morning before going into work and should be repeated whenever possible during the day. Many schools have showering facilities but a useful and perhaps more practical alternative is a nebuliser or steam machine which allows moisture to bathe the vocal folds and reduces dryness in the respiratory tract. Nebulisers are currently available from high street chemists at a reasonably moderate price. It is important to remember that these machines must be cleaned out meticulously after use, as fungal infections can occur if the machines are not properly and hygienically maintained. The use of distilled water is recommended and oils or herbal preparations should not be added to the machines. It has been suggested that maximum benefit is incurred by using it three times a day for five minutes at a time. If you are going to have to give a long presentation or performance then using it immediately beforehand is an excellent anti-abuse preventative measure. Many actors and singers use steam regularly to keep the vocal folds lubricated. The effects of hydration on the vocal folds have been the subject of several published studies (Verdolini-Marston, Sandage and Titze 1994), and show the importance of hydration of the vocal folds. Increased hydration levels will affect the speed and ease with which the folds move, which has an important effect on voice quality. It is also important to remember that in the process of speaking there is a significant amount of heat generated between the vocal folds which increases dryness in addition to the drying properties of overheated classrooms.

Smoking

If at all possible try not to smoke, but if it is impossible to give up then at least try and cut down on the number of cigarettes smoked. Most schools and educational establishments are now smoke free and others offer a separate smoking area, a strategy which is to be encouraged as smoke irritates the respiratory tract and specifically affects the vulnerable vocal folds. Upper respiratory tract irritation and sinus and asthma problems can all be exacerbated by contact with smoky environments.

Diet

Spicy or highly seasoned food can aggravate the mucous membranes of the respiratory tract. It is important to be aware of food or liquid (particularly harmful are spirits such as whisky) which are likely to cause adverse reactions and to avoid them if possible. For those individuals who suffer from gastric reflux (where gastric stomach acid is regurgitated and bathes the laryngeal mucosa causing burning of the larynx, which manifests itself as a reddened and inflamed area near the arytenoid cartilages), it is particularly important to avoid eating late at night. The distance between the upper end of the digestive tract and the larynx is only about 20 cm, which is not very far for gastric acid to travel. One remedy is to sleep with the head raised fairly high; this can be achieved by raising the head of the bed on two bricks, the bedhead should be raised by at least eight inches to guard against the vocally damaging effects of gastric reflux. After a bout of vomiting the vocal folds may be inflamed and can result in a hoarse quality to the voice. Teachers, parents and carers should also be aware that sudden changes in voice quality may indicate a bulimic condition.

Hard attack

A harmful vocal habit is that of hard attack where the vocal folds come together forcefully at the onset of a word beginning with a vowel. There is a lack of coordination between the initiation of voice and the initiation of breath. This is a common characteristic of the speech of a stressed individual and results in a hard initial explosion of sound especially evident in phrases where a number of words begin with vowels such as, 'Alright Class 8, I said quiet!' The explosion of sound that can be heard is caused by the lack of synchronisation of the muscles of breathing and the muscles of speech, resulting in the vocal folds coming together with great force and this may, over a period of time, damage them. If this is an established habit it can be remedied by allowing a little breath through the vocal folds before speaking, for example exercising saying an /h/ before the word 'alright' so that it becomes 'h-alright' takes the stress off the initial sound. Practise lists of words beginning with vowels in this way and once you become familiar with the sensation merely thinking /h/ will be enough. It may be necessary to persevere with exercises of this kind for some time. Chapter 10 gives details of this exercise.

Throat clearing

Throat clearing and coughing are often the presenting symptoms of vocal abuse. Many individuals are quite unaware of how often they cough or clear their throat, but the sensation of having a 'frog in the throat' or a tickle is one that is frequently cited by those with voice problems. Unfortunately the process of 'clearing' the throat has quite the opposite effect. When the individual coughs, the vocal folds are brought together with considerable force. In turn the vocal folds, in an effort to reduce friction, become bathed in mucous which the individual then feels the need to get rid of by clearing the throat, and so the problem continues. One way to limit this is to keep a supply of water available and try to sip some water rather than clear the throat; the action of sipping the water appears to limit the need to clear the throat and gradually the problem becomes less acute. If it is not possible to sip water then try instead to swallow.

Cold remedies

Often teachers in an attempt to avoid taking time off, resort to the use of over-the-counter cold remedies which are designed to eliminate the excess moisture and 'dry up' the cold. These cold remedies contain a high level of caffeine, aspirin and often antihistamine. They are effective if you can go to bed, but if you keep working and speaking, the drying effect upon the vocal tract can only add to the vocal problems. There is always a conflict between taking time off work with what appears to be a rather trivial illness and 'soldiering on', but it is important to remember the damage that can be done by forcing the voice even for short periods. It may be advisable to use paracetamol and not aspirin if you are not well and if you intend to use the voice strenuously at a high volume over a period of time. The blood-thinning properties of aspirin can, in some circumstances, contribute to haemorrhaging of the vocal folds. Likewise sucking throat lozenges and pastilles should be kept to a minimum, as they often contain strong dosages of decongestants, which can affect the vocal tract, likewise mentholated sweets that can be bought over the counter have very limited effect on the mucosal lining and appear to be more of a panacea than a cure.

It is recognised that obviously there are occasions when it is impossible to take time off and so short-term remedial pharmaceutical measures can provide short-term symptom relief, but long-term use is not advised and it cannot be stated too forcibly that any vocal change that persists for longer than two weeks following a cold should be reported to your doctor.

Physical Fitness

The link between voice and physicality has already been explored in Chapter 5, but it is important to remember that keeping flexible and mobile is very important, not only for your long-term health, but also in an effort to underpin and maintain effective respiration, reduce areas of tension and encourage vocal flexibility. Counteracting some of the effects of ageing on the skeletal framework is also to be recommended as effective and efficient use of the voice is possible into old age providing we can maintain supple rib movement to aid respiration and good spine, pelvis and head and neck alignment.

Yoga classes are a particularly useful way in which to focus on relaxation, breathing and general muscular flexibility. Low impact aerobics, as well as encouraging physical fitness will also contribute to increased respiratory function. Keeping fit has the additional benefit of releasing endorphins which influence mood swings and generally are thought to make one feel better, as well as discharging tension. For many people who find exercise classes tedious, a creative alternative form of exercise could be a dance class. If formal classes are not of interest, then regular walking will improve breathing, strengthen muscles and bone, and improve stamina. Swimming will serve the same function and is particularly good for the muscles involved in respiration; swimming has the added benefit of being totally impact free, which is of relevance to the older individual and particularly relevant to those who may have osteoporitic joint conditions.

Warming Up

It is also important to try and remember to warm up vocally before beginning a stressful day's teaching. If we think of athletes warming up before a race, they are rarely seen running on the spot, in fact most perform an initial series of stretching exercises which gently encourage muscle movement and only then do they start to jog or run slowly but never do they run at full stretch as part of their warm up routine. Teachers, however, rarely do anything but the equivalent of running at full speed vocally once they begin work, so to spend time gently vocally stretching and making contact with the breath is important. The vocal warm up exercises included in Chapter 10 are very useful preventative measures against vocal abuse and misuse and are to be recommended.

A strategy for warming up is to involve the children, by doing exercises which both relax and energise you all. This can be as simple as the game of 'Simon says', in which the instruction is only carried out if prefixed by the phrase 'Simon says'. For example, 'Simon says raise your arm', ' Simon says jump up high', 'Simon says stand on tip toe' and so on, to a modified series of exercises which allow the children to move around the room, even if only in designated areas. An all-over stretch is very beneficial and can be incorporated into classroom activities without disrupting the teaching routine. The stretch allows the children to alter their positions, which not only prevents them from getting stiff but at the same time releases tension which might result in the children fidgeting and losing concentration. The stretch in fact re-focuses the children's attention and does not, as might be thought, prove distracting. Remember that postural habits can become fixed during pre-adolescence, so any input reaps the double benefit of helping you and the class. There was a time when physical education in schools actively promoted postural awareness and it is regrettable that this is no longer possible, so any individual effort on the part of the teacher is a bonus for pupils.

Clothing

Classrooms and school premises are extremely difficult to heat to a constant temperature. In the early morning the classroom is usually quite cool, with the temperature warming to a muggy heat by the time the last bell goes. As a result teachers often find that they are cold when they come into school, especially in older schools which are not well insulated. When we are cold, blood vessels contract to maintain as much body heat as possible and cold muscles do not work as efficiently as they do when warm, so we do not relax easily. In an effort to conserve heat we tend to limit movement and we often see individuals 'hugging' themselves to retain body heat. A useful tactic is to wear layers of clothing to school, so that as the room heats up you can divest yourself of a layer and maintain a steady degree of warmth throughout the day. Clothing that is too tight particularly across the chest and back can impede breathing by restricting the degree of rib expansion and in the same way wide belts which are pulled too tight will constrict the diaphragm, particularly when individuals are seated, thereby limiting effective respiration.

Common Classroom Infections

It is useful to check ventilation and if possible bring it up in discussion with other staff members as inadequate ventilation contributes to a hot dry atmosphere which is damaging to the voice and in addition contributes to the spread of infection so that coughs and colds abound. It may be necessary to have a well-documented procedure for minimising the spread of coughs and colds. Teachers could request that children are not sent to school if they are suffering from very heavy colds but if this is not realistic then try and separate the infected from the non-infected to limit cross-infection. Have a plentiful supply of tissues available in the classroom and do encourage children to keep using them, as well as trying to persuade them to cough into the tissue and not over their fellow pupils. This is obviously worse for those teachers who work with small children, but repeated colds can be particularly debilitating and many teachers report that their voice first showed signs of deterioration after a bad cold. If you do catch a bad cold, try and talk as little as possible and look after your voice by drinking plenty of water, steaming and resting your voice. Instead of talking to the children continuously throughout the day, indicate to them that you have a cold and that you need to talk less, rely instead on some of the strategies outlined below to make them aware of the need to look at you and to listen to instructions.

Attention Skills

Small children often have poorly developed listening and attention skills; they may also have problems of audio immaturity and these are areas that teachers often focus on in infant and junior school teaching. Teachers should try to encourage children to look and listen for signals which are not necessarily vocal. It is useful to begin each term and half term with a refresher session where the teacher recaps on the procedures involved in listening and looking. Highlight the importance of the child's active involvement in this process and the need for them to remember to look and listen to the teacher throughout the day without prompting. Asking for the class's attention is a frequent daily occurrence. Rather than having to say or shout this instruction, try using an alternative non-vocal approach, for example a large cardboard hand on a stick with 'Stop' written on it can be raised to indicate that the class must be quiet and await instructions. Cardboard traffic lights on a stick with the red stop light painted a vivid red can be used as well. This encourages children to keep a watching eye on the teacher and is good for working on visual attention. Cymbals and drums can be used to signal silence on the part of the class. When they hear the sound they must stop talking and be quiet. Another useful device is to devise a round robin message which follows a well designated pathway. The teacher gives her request to Child A who is nearby and then this child passes on the message to Child B and so on around the class. Initially the children may make mistakes but by making a game of it and establishing it as an accepted procedure when in good voice, it can be used most effectively when necessary. Ask the last child for the message and compare this with the response of the first child. The class are always anxious to let the last child know if a mistake has been made, but the message can range from 'Be quiet' to 'Put your books away and stand in line'. By making sure that the children realise the importance of listening you can encourage improved listening skills and conserve voice. For teachers with severe voice problems using a hand or throat mike or indeed fashioning a megaphone from cardboard can be a useful aid.

Hearing

Teachers will all be familiar with the problem of hearing impairment in pupils. This can range from a degree of hearing loss which requires hearing aids to intermittent deafness due to recurrent middle ear infection, commonly known as 'glue ear'. For some primary school children this can be a source of continual absence from school and indeed because of the fluctuating nature of middle ear infection a child may be able to hear clearly one day and not the next. Speech and language problems are also relatively common in the primary school population. These can range from problems with language to problems with actually saying specific sounds which is where work on auditory attention is undoubtedly useful as it encourages the child to really concentrate on the auditory rather than the visual channel. Teachers too should have their hearing periodically tested as with age hearing acuity becomes less. Any diminution in hearing may be almost imperceptible from one year to the next but the cumulative effect over many years can make it difficult for teachers to hear pupils or to distinguish what is being said if there are a number of children talking at one time. Teachers who have to listen above the noise of machinery such as drills or saws or indeed home economics teachers who have to listen above the noise of electric beaters or sewing machines will find this particularly difficult if they have any degree of hearing loss. Some hearing loss will also have the effect of making it difficult to self-monitor the loudness level of conversational speech.

Arranging the Classroom

Positioning the class with care is very important. Remember that lip reading is an important additional factor in aiding understanding. We lip read instinctively when listening to speech, which is why so often we need to ask for repetition of specific information on the telephone and why confusion arises and we say on occasion, 's for sun, not f for Freddy'. If pupils can be seated so that they can see the teacher's face when he or she is giving instructions then it will greatly aid understanding and reduce the level of loudness required by the teacher. For male teachers it is important to remember that moustaches and beards do make lip reading more difficult so compensate by articulating clearly. Similarly, when working in acoustically difficult spaces, if children are grouped there will be a damping effect which will lessen the need for excessive volume on the part of the teacher.

Positive Teaching Styles

Arrangement of the classroom should allow for free movement for the pupils and permit the teacher to move freely amongst the class. This allows the teacher to be in physical contact with all the pupils, so that they can stand beside or behind them when teaching and be able to make physical as well as verbal or visual contact with each child. Recent work within the classroom has shown that a teacher can modify 'bad' behaviour by walking up to the child, putting their hand firmly on the child's shoulder, exerting gentle pressure and saying nothing. Nagging wears the students out, and is deeply wearying for teachers, but it seldom changes the student's behaviour. Many teachers recognise their own tendency to nag and also recognise the fruitlessness and negative atmosphere this response creates, but it is difficult to find alternative responses which are effective, hence the frequent physical contact suggestion. It is obviously unadvisable to use any form of pressure that could be interpreted as pushy, jostling or threatening.

Teachers report that their greatest resource is their ability to observe and assess the mood of the class and to remain vigilant without becoming reactive to the class's manipulation. Most teachers find objective observation allows teachers to change the class's behaviour without losing their respect and co-operation. When teachers were questioned, most reported that they found talking, deliberate hindering, idleness and pupils being out of their seats the most annoying aspects of class behaviour, specifically because it is these behaviours that considerably reduced teaching time. Children are quick to observe the teacher's vulnerable areas and some disruptive individuals try to capitalise on these.

It is important to maximise positive response and reinforcement of good behaviour and minimise negative responses. When the negative response is used sparingly, its effectiveness is considerable; when used constantly the effectiveness is minimised. Many teachers questioned admitted that their reinforcement of positive attitudes to academic standards far outweighed their positive attitudes to social behaviour. When social behaviour is worthy of positive reinforcement, it is important that it is given, otherwise lack of effort is associated with positive reinforcement in a negative way, in other words lack of effort is commented on, while praise is sometimes withheld from pupils who continue gamely to do what they are told without causing any trouble. Positive reinforcement should be used with honesty so that children see it as genuine and well deserved; they quickly see through 'phoney' praise and this therefore invalidates real effort. Approval and disapproval is very important to children and approval should not be 'reserved' for really major effort, instead disapproval should be limited and if possible used in very specific circumstances. It is often much more common and easier to catch children doing the wrong thing and be disapproving than to catch them doing the appropriate thing. More is achieved if you can catch them doing the right thing and give praise.

Negotiation Skills

A major cause of stress develops as a result of poor negotiation within the classroom setting or within the staffroom. A great deal of tension can be defused by the application of effective negotiation strategies. A major cause of adolescent rebellion and staff discontent comes about through the frustration that results when individuals find themselves in 'no win' situations. The old style authoritarian approach places people in the position of feeling that if one person wins the other loses. Negotiations that work to find 'win/win' agreements (where both sides feel they have won) rather than 'win/lose' situations leave everyone happy and as a result productive and co-operative. Young people who are, quite rightly, being taught to 'know their rights' often have difficulty understanding that other people also have the same rights, problems and needs. On one hand they are told to 'be assertive' and 'learn to say no'; on the other they are accused of being 'self- centred' and 'stubborn'. Assertiveness, when it does not take the needs of others into consideration, becomes a form of bullying. It takes maturity to be able to find the workable solution to problems that seem unresolvable. Most adolescents have a highly developed sense of justice and can therefore relate to the fairness of the 'win/win' negotiation.

In order to bring about such an agreement it is necessary to break through the deadlock that is the result of individuals being unwilling to accept the other person's point of view. Concessions often need to be made and these should be made on both sides. When one party is expected to concede too much without due recognition and discussion of their needs, the result is a breakdown in communication, feelings of resentment and a withdrawal of goodwill. Such situations benefit neither party and only serve to increase general stress levels.

Negotiation skills can be learned from books or better still by the organisation of a staff development or in-service workshop. The information gleaned from such training can be passed on to students by the application of strategies to the classroom situation and formally within the oral element of the English class. Many schools have Personal and Social Skills classes and these skills could be usefully shared in such an arena. Schools with specific problems such as bullying and racism can apply the principles of 'win/win' negotiation in order to bring about understanding and reconciliation. The teacher who is able to apply the principles of fair negotiation to a difficult discipline problem could find she not only solves the specific problem, but by a change in tactics alters the atmosphere of the classroom for the better and indeed influences the group culture within the school. While a confrontational situation exists there will be no winners and the teacher's voice will suffer.

For many teachers the most difficult time to maintain discipline is as the children come in and go out of the classroom. It is worthwhile trying to keep the children outside the door for a little longer and to give the instruction at that time; for example, 'go in quietly, sit at your desk and get out your books', rather than trying to give the instruction as they come into the classroom when the level of noise is much higher and teachers have to fight against this to make themselves heard.

Teachers questioned for a television programme were very aware of the good day/bad day syndrome and were able to voice opinions as to why these occur. There was agreement that negative responses tend to occur when teachers are ill prepared for the class, or unsure of their material, or when they were under external and personal stress. Teachers recognised that their mood was often dictated by a wide variety of situations, but it was particularly important to allow sufficient recovery time from a previous situation. If, for example, there was a lack of recovery time from the effect of family tensions, a difficult journey to school, an unpleasant incident in the previous lesson, or from an early morning staffroom rush, then this could impinge on the entire school day.

It is important to remember to try and break this type of pattern or at least to be aware of situations that can precipitate it and if possible make changes, allowing more recovery time. Of paramount importance for the teacher is the need to recognise that on occasions it is important to delegate activities, to admit to needing help and to try to use all possible means to reduce areas of tension within one's working environment. May we suggest that as part of your Health and Safety at work procedures you make sure that all teachers have access to the following information.

Voice care

In order to avoid misusing or abusing your voice the following information may be helpful:

- Do not try to talk above loud background noise at social or sports events or above machinery noise.
- Avoid smoking.
- Avoid chemical irritants or dusty conditions.
- Try to keep alcoholic drinks to a minimum.
- Do not respond by shouting when upset or anxious.
- Avoid excessive use of the telephone.
- Spicy foods and dairy products may affect your voice.
- The voice is closely linked with emotion – tension or depression will be reflected in the voice.
- The voice needs moisture. Keep up your liquid intake but avoid excess alcohol which dehydrates.
- Pale-coloured urine indicates a good level of hydration.

- Warm up the voice gently before prolonged speaking.
- Avoid dry atmospheres. Use a humidifier or water spray to moisten the air in centrally-heated classrooms, offices or homes. If you have conventional radiators a wet towel draped over the radiator effectively humidifies the air.
- If your voice is hoarse or you are losing your voice do not whisper or try to continue talking; rest your voice.
- Be aware of voice quality. Monitor any change in your voice carefully and see a doctor if there is a persistent change in quality.
- If you are having continuing vocal problems ask your doctor to refer you to an ear, nose and throat specialist or otolaryngologist.

Acoustics

The rooms, halls and other spaces such as lecture theatres, drama studios and laboratories vary tremendously in size and design. The teacher may find that he or she is having to spend the whole day in one space, a situation common in the primary school, or that he or she works in a variety of spaces, each of which creates its own specific acoustic. Teachers and lecturers in the secondary and tertiary sector find the latter situation to be the norm.

The structure of buildings and the materials used inside them determine the ultimate acoustic quality. Acoustic science is extremely complicated and a detailed knowledge is not necessary for the teacher. There are, however, simple guidelines that can assist the speaker in the use, and if necessary, the alteration or adaptation of the space. It is advisable to observe the size and shape of the room, the texture of the flooring, the height and shape of the ceilings and what the ceiling surface consists of. Note the number and position of windows and other glass surfaces, the material used for window and door frames, the presence of wooden or steel beams, the furnishings (steel or wooden cupboards), chairs and the substances used to cover walls such as the texture of paint, notice boards, drapes, posters, curtains, pull blinds or venetian blinds.

Generally speaking (and obviously all manner of combinations exist and operate differently in different spaces), low ceilings, carpeted floors, covered walls and soft furnishings tend to 'dampen and deaden' sound and tend to absorb the voice, making it more necessary to actively voice consonants and pitch the voice slightly higher.

Hard surfaces such as varnished timber or wooden tiles, steel-framed windows and doors, large expanses of glass and bare walls tend to produce a bright, sharp and occasionally echoing sound. This sometimes requires a change in pitch (a lower pitch sometimes helps) and a slower pace, as the reverberation of the sound can interfere with the next sound, making speech indistinct.

Both these extremes, the 'dead' one and the 'bright' one, tend to be difficult to work in. Teachers complain that working in a difficult acoustic just adds to the feeling of hard work. They feel their voices are swallowed up by the 'dead' sound and the trap they fall into is to push the voice and consequently they end up feeling vocally tired. From the student's point of view the consonants, which carry the meaning of words, can be lost and therefore intelligibility is decreased. In such circumstances particular attention paid to the consonants will make a difference. A small benefit for the teacher is that classes can sound slightly quieter as the acoustic absorbs classroom noise as well.

In the brighter acoustic teachers complain of being distracted by the reverberation and this proves to be very tiring for both teacher and class. A bright sound is exacerbated by a large area, as any teacher knows if she has attempted to have a band or orchestra rehearsal or a choral verse rehearsal in a large echoing space. The reverberation can make timing extremely difficult and any space used for such purposes should be adapted by the installation of absorbent tiles and/or lowered ceilings.

Modification of a difficult space is not always easy and where cost is going to be incurred professional advice should be sought. There are however certain inexpensive adaptations that can be made.

If the room is 'dead' try:

- Remove any materials such as coats (hanging on pegs) and unnecessary notice boards.
- Consider removing the carpet, provided of course that the floor surface is reasonable.
- If walls are lined with books, move them out of the room if possible.

If the room is 'over-bright' try:

- Introducing screens made of an absorbent material (egg trays do a good job).
- Covering the floor with a soft surface such as cork tiles, carpets or a soft vinyl.

- Lowering the ceiling or padding the ceiling (egg trays again!).
- Introducing more absorbent material such as drapes and book shelves.
- Cover walls in mounted art work.

When working in large spaces teachers encounter problems unrelated to design, but related to the natural loss of sound over distance. Sound waves decrease in strength as they move away from the point at which they are initiated. At a distance of 20 feet (6 m) sounds are only 25% as strong as they were at a distance of 10 feet (3 m). At a distance of 40 feet from the source, the sounds are only 6.25% as strong as at a distance of 10 feet (Hann 1979).

In order to prevent the loss of the power of sound it is important to decrease the size of the space by sectioning off the teaching area, using reflecting screens. The typical gym hall found in sixth form colleges and secondary schools is often used for a number of activities. When touring theatre companies perform in leisure centres, school halls and other non-theatre venues they generally transport a staging area that has a false ceiling. This ensures that the acoustic they experience each night is not too badly affected by the ever-changing environment. False ceilings do not produce an ideal acoustic but are nevertheless very effective. They are obviously not cheap and prices vary according to size. An acoustic adviser or sound engineer should always be consulted before any construction of this type is considered; they will be able to give an independent opinion as to the most effective modification. Remember parents are a wonderful resource; there may be an expert associated with the school.

When working in any space with a difficult acoustic it is always advisable to consider the students' ability to support what they hear with information gleaned from what they see. There is an element of lip reading in all the understanding we extract from speech, provided of course that the speaker is seen. In the theatre it is well known that a production that is inadequately lit is more difficult to hear, as is one in which the staging of 'theatre in-the-round' means that the audience does not view the actors from the front, but is presented with a profile or a back view. Problems of this type can be caused by poor sight-lines in the auditorium and similar situations can occur in teaching spaces. The problem can occur when classrooms are wide and not sufficiently deep. Concentration and understanding will always be limited by too oblique a view. The chances of hearing are always improved when visibility is good. This visual feedback also plays a significant role in listening to speech over a background of noise; you will remember the sensation of communicating with someone in a tube or railway station, or in a noisy pub. In these circumstances the lips, tongue and facial muscles and gesture communicate meaning. Very little volume is used as strain often results if volume is used over high levels of sound.

A useful aspect of the actor's work involves the need to work in theatre in-the-round. This involves areas of the audience having to listen without the benefit of seeing the actor's face, a situation that often occurs in the classroom. The techniques used by actors to overcome this problem involve an omni-directional awareness of the entire audience and a mental communication with them. Technically concentrating on final consonants and consonants in general is usually beneficial. We traditionally communicate face to face but should not disregard the communicative potential of the whole body.

Chapter 9
Beyond the
Teaching Role

The vocal demands on the teacher are not confined to those encountered in the classroom. In addition the teacher may be expected to undertake the following duties.

The teacher as orator

This means addressing the assembly, leading the prayers, giving the moral speech, conveying the daily information to the assembled school, being prepared to address a governors' meeting, welcoming the audience to a play, or music evening and possibly addressing a gathering of parents on matters pertaining to the children's education, such as changes in education policy, choosing secondary education and fund raising.

If you have to give speeches you will need to take the time to prepare yourself well. It is no good hoping that when the time comes you will be able to 'come up with something'. The terror of having to speak is halved the moment you prepare. When you are confident your voice will behave normally, obviously a little tension or 'stage fright' is absolutely natural, and even useful as it sharpens the wits. Teachers should remember that what they do all day, every day, is to address groups; it is what they are good at, nevertheless it is very impressive when someone stands up and gives an effective speech. If in doubt, use a clearly defined note structure, along the lines of a composition structure, have a beginning, a middle and an end. As a useful 'rough' measure, the middle of your talk should carry 60% of your message, the beginning and end 20% each. It is a great aid to both speaker and listener if you can signal the main points and develop a framework which contains the focus of the speech. Obviously the skills of oratory are specialised ones and much has been written which will help those who wish to extent their competence in this area. At the most simplistic level, the recommendation to 'tell them what you're going to tell them, tell them and then tell them what you've told them' is valuable.

Often the duty is to welcome a speaker, or to thank one, so it is advisable to do some research beforehand. Find out who the speaker is and include their achievements in your introduction. If your duty is to thank them, make notes during the speech and reiterate the salient and most memorable points. Even an informal occasion such as an address by a guest speaker can produce considerable tension in the individual who has to officiate. The voice can feel as if it has 'seized up' in these moments of pressure. The question is what can you do to help yourself? The answer is, quite a lot.

Firstly make sure you have practised your speech a number of times, preferably to a real audience, a partner, or a colleague if possible. It is important to speak it aloud, and not just go over it in your head. If you must, use a tape recorder, but without an audience you may be inclined to listen to yourself, rather than communicating with your audience.

When practising, make sure you are standing well, with the weight distributed across both feet. If you lose alignment and shift the weight, the immediate impression is one of being ill at ease. When you stand firmly, but without tension, you not only look better, you feel more in control.

If there is a microphone available, and you wish to use it, then do so, but not before you have tested it and made sure it works. Tapping and asking whether you can be heard is disconcerting for you and your audience and can destroy your confidence. It is important that you have a trial run and know how to position yourself in relation to the microphone and know what volume is acceptable. Nothing is worse than 'blasting' the audience, or thinking you are being amplified when you are not.

Do not take a lot of papers up onto the podium. The danger here is that you may lose your notes amongst other papers and worse still, that you may drop them. Most importantly, do not learn your speech 'parrot fashion', as you may forget it and not be able to pick up where you stopped. When you speak, speak *to* your audience not *at* them, make eye contact and allow pauses so that significant points can be digested. Above all allow the voice to inflect and move naturally. Remember the odd slip is not the end of the world, the audience knows you are human.

The teacher as sports coach

This includes working out of doors in all weathers, shouting to encourage the team, issuing instructions and cautioning unruly behaviour. It could include teaching swimming in a large indoor pool with a very poor acoustic; being a cricket umpire during the hayfever season; teaching physical education, gym, dance or aerobics and having to speak while demonstrating. A problem produced by the need to vocalise whilst exercising is that less breath support can be given to the voice when lying down than when standing up and much of the aerobic and gym teachers' work is demonstration led and floor work predominates. The number of aerobic exercise teachers who experience voice problems is high and far outweighs that of dance teachers.

Sports duties are likely to present the most vocal challenges. The cold of the rugby, soccer or netball pitch is a problem because when people are cold, they tend to raise their shoulders and tighten the neck and jaw, pull back their head and fold their arms across their body. This physical position is not conducive to easy efficient voice production. The open space is another problem. There are no hard vibrating surfaces for sound to bounce off, so the voice fades as it travels over the distance and as a result the teacher shouts. Shouting in itself is not a problem, it is after all a natural activity, children shout joyously in the playground, but unfortunately the 'art of shouting' is something many adults in the western world have lost. In many cultures shouting is still commonplace, but for us it is often related to anger or frustration. In Chapter 11 we look at healthy shouting, and for anyone who needs to project loudly over distances out of doors, it is well worth learning.

Some helpful suggestions when using the voice on the field are:

- If possible use a megaphone. They are easy to make with a piece of cardboard. If this is not possible, cup the hand around the mouth and try to 'call' rather than shout.
- Remember that you are involved in a sport and not a war. Keep your sense of humour and you are more likely to keep your voice. In laughter the voice is wonderfully free, you will have noticed the difference you feel when your team suddenly makes a brilliant move after playing abysmally, your joyous 'Yes!' is very different from the former exasperated 'Come on!'
- Keep warm by wearing warm clothing, scarfs and gloves; if necessary, also run around until you get warm. When coaching,

take your team near to a wall or keep them close to you so that you can use a more conversational voice level.

• When the wind is blowing you are unlikely to be easily audible. Do not battle against the wind; the children seldom hear anyway. If you can attract their attention they are more likely to understand you if you mouth clearly. Use a control, such as a whistle, or flags, or develop your own semaphore that is understood by the children.

The teacher who has to teach swimming has the least enviable job! The acoustics in indoor pools are invariably poor, because of the abundance of hard surfaces and high ceilings. Often they are echo chambers and the space becomes incredibly noisy, particularly if the classes take place while public or shared sessions are occurring.

It is difficult to offer helpful advice here, as many teachers say that it is the most difficult task and that it causes enormous vocal tiredness. Some teachers have said that once they have improved their general voice production techniques and found non-verbal ways of controlling the group they have been able to cope better. As with field sports, the use of a control to minimise voice use is important; whistles can be high-pitched enough to pierce the noisy acoustic, although problems occur if other teachers use them in shared sessions. Using a flag to get children to swim to the side can be effective, but often a sound signal will be needed as well. A variety of signals should be taught to the children, for example one long blast means 'stop', two short blasts means 'come to the side'.

Small children and non-swimmers should only be taught in a quiet environment and in small groups. All children should be clearly instructed on what to do when they have completed a length, so that they look to the teacher for advice before proceeding. It is pointless to expect children to hear anything when their heads are in the water.

Watch your posture as you lean towards the swimmers. Bend from the knees rather than leaning from the waist. Wear suitable comfortable clothing and shoes.

When organising galas, remember that even children, who seldom lose their voices, can be hoarse after a gala. This is because the noise rebounds off the hard surfaces and swimmers and supporters find themselves shouting louder and louder in order to hear themselves. All that those in the water hear is a roar of sound. It is in this highly competitive atmosphere that problems can occur. The usual advice about drinking large quantities of water apply here too, as pools are usually overheated. If possible let another teacher keep discipline on the bus going back to school; you will deserve the rest.

The teacher as entertainer

This can involve performing as the disc jockey at a noisy disco, calling the dances at a fund-raising barn dance, making the public address announcements at fetes, and performing, often unwillingly, at leavers' parties! Of all these activities the most vocally dangerous is to shout above the noise of the disco; a microphone should always be used in such instances. If entertaining is really not your forte avoid being forced into it by offering to contribute in another way.

The teacher as thespian

Untrained teachers may find themselves conducting the drama club, or even teaching GCSE drama, producing a class or drama festival play, or in its most basic, but by no means simplest form, reading and telling stories to groups of younger pupils. Drama classes are, by their very nature, highly participatory and noisy and should be controlled by means of a non-verbal signal, such as a tambourine.

Although the purpose of a drama class is to develop and encourage verbal communication between pupils it also develops co-operative skills. By focusing on interpersonal communication and mutual support the group can avoid the chaos that results from drama classes that simply expend energy. When a degree of ensemble work develops the drama class works best and both pupils and teachers enjoy the experience. A word of advice for the inexperienced director: avoid taking on a full-length production in the primary school as these tend to be too long for children to sustain an interest in, either as performers or as audience. Parents also find extra rehearsals and long evenings difficult if younger children are involved. Professional child actors are not allowed to be on stage for more than two hours – perhaps the same unwritten law should apply to school productions. It is also important to enlist parental and staff support with regard to organisation and assistance and to delegate from the outset. In primary schools the theme programme allows participation from other departments such as music, art and gym and provides involvement from a broad range of children, not just the best actors. Parents do not expect to see 'professional' standards in a school production and much of the charm lies in the unexpected 'hiccup'.

The Teacher as reader

Most teachers read aloud well and enjoy doing so, but there are a significant number for whom this is a daunting and often vocally tiring task. There are those who 'feel the throat tighten' as they read and hear a voice produced that they find difficult to recognise as their own; others feel inhibited and self-conscious when having to entertain or be seen to be performing. The close link between 'theatre' and the classroom is recognised by many and for some it is an element they really feel happy about. There are those who are natural communicators and there are those who feel they did not enter teaching to be 'performers'.

The teachers who are most likely to find themselves in the position of having to read to a class regularly are the pre-primary, infant and primary school teachers, as well as teachers of English literature and other humanities subjects and those whose duties include reading at assembly. Teachers of the younger age groups expect to read aloud regularly, but teachers who find themselves with a class they did not originally train for are often worried about how effectively they 'tell the story', and it is when there is anxiety over the reading that the voice is likely to become over-used and tired. Some PGCE-trained teachers who find themselves in a position of having to read aloud have said that their one-year course did not provide the practice they feel they needed to read to a class as well as they would wish.

Teachers are all knowledgeable about the rudiments of reading and so there is no need to reiterate them here. That there is a significant difference between fluent reading and the art and skill of reading aloud to an audience is not often acknowledged. The most important of these differences is that the reader has the book in front of them and can follow the printed word, while the audience cannot, therefore the audience is at a considerable disadvantage and must be helped to 'enter the world of the story'. The art of the teacher who reads to the class is the important art of the story-teller, and this, sadly, is an art being lost to our culture – or rather replaced by television and video. In the lives of many children, the primary school teacher is the only adult who ever reads to them. The classroom 'story' takes on enormous importance for children who are not lucky enough to be read to in the home. Obviously all teachers want to read aloud to the best of their ability because they want children to be stimulated and excited by words and language and to be inspired to read avidly for themselves.

Here are some simple suggestions that can make a considerable difference to the ease and quality of reading aloud.

1. Remember that any speech has to be heard, decoded and understood before the audience can react to it, so it is important that you allow the audience time and space to go through the listening process and therefore to share in the process of story-telling by engaging their imaginations and formulating images of the language as they receive it.

2. Younger children need to be close to the reader so as to be able to participate in the two-way process of the story. But whatever their age, bringing your class closer to you, when possible, will save you having to over-use the voice as well as improve your chances of reading *to* them rather than *at* them. A percentage of children may have undetected hearing problems and as we all 'hear' to some degree by lip reading, encourage listeners to look at you. Give them both physical and audible information by allowing your face and body to convey the story, meeting their eyes when appropriate and shaping the sounds of speech with the lips and tongue. When a reader is committed to the story and to the telling of it, these aspects generally fall into place.

3. Even before you speak you are having some effect on the listeners. Whether this effect is positive or negative is dependent on the body language you use. At best the body should be alert but relaxed as any unwanted excess tension will transfer itself to the voice, and make sure your chair is comfortable and that you have a glass of water close at hand. The class, too, should be comfortable and should avoid slumping onto desks. Story-telling should be a two-way communication process with listening being as important as reading or speaking.

4. As mentioned before, eye contact is needed in order to relate to the listeners. It also helps to indicate phrases and to emphasise specific words so as to keep the feeling that the story is being told, not just read. For some teachers making eye contact while reading is 'easier said than done'. The usual comment is that the teacher is afraid of losing the place, which can easily happen in text tightly packed onto the page. When reading anything as complicated as Dickens or even Mark Twain, the advice is to scan the chapter first and to become familiar with it. If you know exactly what you are going to read and when, for example if you are going to read a religious

extract at an assembly, photocopy and if necessary enlarge the extract and use a highlighter to mark the words following the phrase you look up on; this will help you come back to the right place. For the listeners, 'looking up' can be annoying if it is done without reason. Readers sometimes look up with alarming regularity because they have been led to believe that any eye contact represents good reading practice. They do not make eye contact with sincerity but rather flick their eyes over the listeners before returning hurriedly to the text. The golden rule is only to look up when it is appropriate and makes meaningful contact. It is also important to be aware of the whole class, not just a section of it. The eye contact you make with the class should allow you time to include them and should allow them time to digest what you have just said. Occasionally you may want to repeat a phrase or a word from the text in order to increase the level of the group's involvement in your story, but remember they do not have the text in front of them, nor are they able to cast their eyes ahead and anticipate the story as you are. Unless the reader makes contact with the class, they may as well have listened to the radio. The value for the class lies in being read to by an adult they know and can relate to.

5.   Most people reading aloud read at a faster pace than they realise. We are not very good at monitoring the speed at which we are reading or speaking, particularly if we are under pressure and do not naturally enjoy the delivery of words. The reader's greatest asset is their ability to give themselves and their audience time. The audience needs time to digest one idea before being fed with another, they need to be able to hear how one idea develops into the next so that they can build up the progression of ideas and be involved in the development of the narrative. They also need time to 'take on board' new characters, often with unusual names, and to build up, from the language that they hear, a visual image as well as formulating a response to the incidents and emotions. A slower speech rate also helps the reader, as it allows for eye contact, changes of vocal tone for different characters, the building up of an imaginative response to the text and, if the reader does not know the story, it allows them to go through their own 'see, decode, understand and react' process.

6.   The ability to scan ahead is something that can be improved by practice and confidence. Often it is the panic of losing the

place that prevents an otherwise confident sight-reader from letting the eyes glide over the page. A most useful exercise is to hold a closed book in front of you; open it suddenly; let the eyes fall onto a phrase; close the book; look up and speak the phrase. At first the eyes flicker frantically over the page and have to be encouraged to settle on a phrase. If this is done regularly it builds ability and confidence and is an excellent exercise to do with children from 9 years onwards. It begins to extend the eye's peripheral vision and it is this that allows us to take in the full sense of phrases and improves choppy, broken reading. It is great fun and can be practised first using lists of phrases and idioms, as they are less daunting than great blocks of text. Progression can then be made onto more densely blocked text, using books that have larger writing and good spacing.

The teacher as tour guide

This can include conducting tours to museums, giving information on the dinosaur while counting heads, or traipsing across battlefields, battling against the wind and cold and projecting the voice, while describing the action. This could also include skiing trips, sports tours, and a week's educational field trip abroad. In these instances the teacher is having to use the voice at high volume for long periods of time in adverse circumstances. As with the field sports teachers, draw the group around you to avoid having to project in the noise of a busy tourist centre, and encourage children to always position themselves in a semi-circle around you, so that they are all able to see you. Remember even when they are close up to you in an echoing cathedral, they will be doing a degree of lip reading.

Reduce the fear of losing pupils by making sure you have an excess of adult supervision so that if your duty at a given time is to act as a guide, you are not at the same time responsible for head counts. (A useful way of head counting is to insist that primary school children wear identical school hats.)

The teacher as music teacher

This can also involve singing classes. For men teaching singing in the primary school, problems can arise, as the teacher often has to sing at a pitch far higher than his natural one; we encountered several male teachers who found this problematic and 'tiring'. Male teachers sometimes have difficulty sustaining high pitch for long periods of time, especially those who work with junior schoolchildren or in girls' schools. If you can easily use falsetto do so, but if it creates tension for you to reach the high notes then avoid it. You can use another instrument such as a recorder to suggest the note.

Singing and music teachers often suffer from postural problems if they are not aware of good positioning at the piano or while bending over seated children playing recorders. Make sure your alignment over the piano is healthy; avoid standing and leaning over to play while at the same time looking up at the class and attempting to sing. This also applies to situations that involve playing while looking over your shoulder at a class. If at all possible position the instrument so that you can use the best possible physical position.

Practise what you preach. If you are telling the class to breathe, make sure you are taking the time to breathe yourself. Remember to teach children that the breath should be low and deep. Most children remember choir teachers saying 'Take a big breath' which invariably ends up being a breath which results in raised shoulders. This allows far less intake of breath than a breath taken low in the body, using the lower ribs, diaphragm and abdominal muscles. Keep your shoulders relaxed; playing the piano and string instruments can be conducive to shoulder tension, for example the physical position for violinists can lead to a thrusted head and neck position and it is therefore important to monitor this. If you teach in the lunch period, as many music teachers do, try to make sure you have had your allotted break, don't rush from one class into another. If you demonstrate to the class, do not do so when you are suffering from a cold and do not speak or sing over the noise of the class, instead signal to them to stop first.

The teacher as counsellor

Although all teachers have to participate in parent evenings, some find it an extremely stressful occasion because it almost always follows on after a full day's teaching. While most parents are usually concerned about their children, they are generally good natured, but occasionally they can be defensive or even aggressive. While assaults are uncommon, the pressure on the teacher is enormous and the effect upon an already tired and stressed individual is considerable.

- Try to make sure you have a proper break between the usual working day and the timetabled parent consultations.

- Take time for a quiet cup of tea on your own before calling in the next set of parents, if your system allows it, otherwise keep a drink at hand. Ideally, tea-breaks should be scheduled into an evening of consultations.
- Make sure you are sitting comfortably and not straining over the table or the space between you and the parents. Check your head and shoulder position.
- Do not allow yourself to become defensive. Be honest but polite to parents but do not be intimidated.
- Position chairs at an easy distance from you so that raising your voice is unnecessary.

The worst scenario for teachers is when more than one teacher shares the same space for consultations, as this can become very noisy. The good point about this situation is that time-limits are controlled by a bell that is rung so you do not have trouble 'getting rid' of parents once their time is up.

- Plan your consultation, so that you have opening and closing statements that signal clearly that the consultation is over. Possible phrases to use are, 'Well it's been good to talk to you/meet you, and I will contact you if the situation doesn't seem to improve,' or, 'Thank you for coming and please congratulate John on the effort he has made.'
- Standing up and offering a hand will also signal that the interview is over.

These are just some of the additional duties and requirements demanded of the teacher. Obviously some teachers are not going to become involved in all or any of these roles. In larger schools there are likely to be specialists in each area, but from time to time a teacher finds that a new job makes unusual demands or that in order to take promotion they will have to widen their field of activities. Teachers moving into head teacher posts or head of year posts are going to have to take on many of the duties mentioned.

Personality is a significant factor, because not every teacher is willing to face the wider audience. They feel happy to teach 15-year-old 'tearaways' but are daunted by their far more generous parents. Some teachers enter the profession because they enjoy the links between teaching and the public role. There is a large professional cross-over between teachers and actors and teachers and people who originally considered entering the church. Others love to teach but hate to perform and feel very strongly that, when they entered the profession, these peripheral demands were never made clear to them. Unfortunately, without the willingness to perform at least some of these duties effectively, career prospects may be limited. One way of getting round the problem is not to allow yourself to be persuaded to undertake a commitment you really do not want to be burdened with. We are aware of a school secretary who was finally persuaded to produce the infant school play because no one else was prepared to. Most teachers are willing to give up some of their free time but they are often persuaded, for the sake of the children, to take on additional duties in spite of their overcrowded schedules. Someone has to coach the netball team, someone else has to organise the play or the Christmas concert and if it is your class that is due to visit Calais, then you are going to be the guide. It is important to ensure that whenever possible the additional duties are equally distributed across the staff; very often it is the same people who take on additional duties, year after year.

Chapter 10
Practical Work

This chapter offers a variety of exercises, which have a broad application to all voice users. Some will, by their nature, be more appropriate to class situations but many offer a firm foundation for general voice use. The exercises aim to establish an integrated physical and vocal approach. Some exercises are for specific muscles, others offer a planned sequence of exercises or routines for the voice. Regular periods of exercise are preferable to occasional long sessions and therefore these routines are designed to last for between 10 and 20 minutes.

The exercises raise awareness of habitually held tension in muscles, the placement of the breath and encourage efficient use of energy in body and voice. Habits of any sort are difficult to change and often develop out of the individual's personality and his or her reaction to situations, making it difficult for the individual to be objective about where and how tension is held, and therefore working with another person can be helpful. The way in which people like to work is also highly individual; in recognition of that, we have included a variety of approaches so that if one approach does not appeal another may. If the vocal problem is a recurring one, we would strongly advise seeking professional help before starting on an exercise plan. These exercises will help maintain a healthy voice and prevent problems caused by inappropriate breath and physical alignment, but should never be seen as a substitute for voice therapy if that is required. The participative value of voice work within the classroom has already been stressed, so we have also included exercises that can be done with primary and secondary classes.

Posture Exercises

1a.   Stand as badly as you can (you can involve adolescent classes in this exercise) with the weight on one foot, not two, the ribs compressed, the arms folded across the body, the shoulders raised, the head and neck slumped forwards and the spine curved. Notice how the eye level has fallen.

1b.   Now move from this posture into a more balanced and open position with the weight over both feet; drop the arms to the sides, lengthen the spine, open the rib cage, lower the shoulders and balance the head on the top of the spine. Notice where the eye level is now. Do not over-correct.

2.   Once you are in the balanced position with the knees relaxed and flexible, the pelvis level and not tilted either forwards or backwards, you can begin to stretch. Lift the arms above the head and stretch through the arm to the tips of the fingers while reaching for the ceiling. Look up at the ceiling while you stretch. Keep the feet on the floor and do not lose your balance. The stretch can be maintained for up to thirty seconds before you slowly lower your arms. As you begin the lowering process, allow the head to lower too. The weight of the head and shoulders will take the spine into a curve and the movement will eventually involve bending over at the waist and allowing the knees to bend until the body is completely bent over with the arms swinging loosely, touching the floor. Once in this position make sure the head is free and allowed to hang loosely.

Gradually begin to uncurl, by building up one vertebra upon the next until the spine begins to unfold and lengthen. Leave the shoulders, head and neck until last. Once you are completely, but not rigidly upright, repeat the exercise a second and third time.

A word of caution: moving to an upright position too quickly can occasionally lead to a momentary feeling of dizziness, so uncurl the spine slowly.

Shoulder Exercises

1.   Lift the shoulders up to the ears, hold this position for 5 seconds and then release. Repeat twice more.

2.   Lift the shoulders up to the ears then move them backwards so that the shoulder blades almost meet. Hold them in this position briefly, before releasing them and moving them forward and upward again. Continue the cycle for at least six rotations.

3.   Raise the right arm above the head, stretching through the

arm to the fingertips. Notice how the rib cage opens in this position. Take the arm backwards, breathing out as it descends and then complete the circle by lifting the arm up back to the starting point as breath flows back into the body. Repeat this exercise three times on the right side, taking care never to hold the breath.

4. Repeat the same exercise with the left arm, making sure you co-ordinate the breath with the action. (Breathe in as the arm is lifted and breathe out as the arm is lowered.)

Another useful exercise can be found in the routine for secondary schools later in this chapter.

Neck Exercises

When working on the neck it is important to avoid fully rotating the head. Neck work should be gentle and should not place stress on the vertebrae. Extending the length of the neck should not be a forceful movement. Try to imagine that someone is gently brushing a hand along the surface of the neck and 'think' the length of the neck rather than physically stretching it. Additional neck exercises are included in Chapter 5.

1. Beginning with the head in a balanced position, slowly drop the chin down onto the chest, feeling the extension of the muscles at the back of the neck. Do this three to six times, making sure that no movement is forced. Return the head to a balanced position and feel the length in the neck at the back.

2. Keeping the feeling of length in the back of the neck, but not over-extending it, take the head to the right shoulder and then keeping the chin close to the chest, move the head slowly to the left shoulder. Repeat starting at the left shoulder and moving towards the right one. Never rotate the head fully, or do any neck exercises hurriedly.

3. Keeping the head balanced on the top of the spine, alternately lift and sway the shoulders in a 'wave-like' motion. Keep the movement fluid and relaxed.

4. Using the image of the head balanced on a greasy ball-bearing at the top of the spine, allow the head to bob gently from the right shoulder to the left shoulder using gentle movements rather like those of a marionette.

Relaxation Exercises

There are two very effective methods of relaxing on your own. The first is through a 'stretch and release' method and the second is through the use of image and the establishment of a feeling of release in the muscles you are able to isolate. For most people the tensions they carry become habitual and therefore are difficult to isolate and to identify in specific muscles.

Stretching

1. Kneel on the floor, sit back on your heels and then stretch the arms forward along the floor, so that you feel the stretch in the spine. Hold the stretch for a few seconds and then release it.

2. Lie on the floor with arms and legs in a star shape. Now stretch diagonally, so that the right arm and left leg are stretched away from the centre of the body. Hold then release. Then stretch the left arm and the right leg. Hold then release. Feel the sense of breadth in the back.

3. You can do this exercise either sitting in a chair or lying on the floor. If in a chair make sure you are comfortable with sufficient support for your neck and lower back. If lying on the floor you may want to place a book under your head and bend your legs at the knee in order to reduce the curve in the lower back. In this exercise you issue instructions to yourself, beginning with the command to 'hold tension', then to release it and then finally to assess the new muscle state. The aim of the exercise is to teach the body to differentiate between habitually held tension and the released state.

3a. Starting with the head, push it into the floor or the back of the chair. Hold the tension. Release the tension and then assess the different sensations in the muscles of the neck and those around them.

3b. Now push the shoulder girdle into the back of the chair or the floor. Give the self-instructed command 'hold'. After a few seconds self-instruct to 'release'. Thirdly, 'assess' the difference between the states of tension and release.

3c. Move on to the back. Push the spine into the floor or into the back of the chair. Hold the tension and then release and assess.

3d. Continue through the body, tightening and releasing buttocks, arms, fists, legs, feet, jaw and finally the whole body.

Image relaxation

Once more get comfortable either on a chair or on the floor. Make sure you are warm. Think of a place you would like to be, imagine somewhere tranquil such as a warm beach, in a field of flowers or on a gently rocking boat on a blue sea. Use the image to create a feeling of peace. Imagine the feeling of the sun on your limbs. If possible play some relaxing music. Concentrate on the feeling that in this ideal setting you have no responsibilities or worries. Try to recreate the experience of being on holiday.

Now work through the body from the feet upwards, ensuring that each part of the body is relaxed. If you are not happy with the state of tension in a group of muscles, tighten the muscles in question and then release them. Work up slowly through the legs, pelvis and buttocks, spine, rib cage, chest, shoulders and arms, hands, fingers, neck, head and facial muscles.

Breathing Exercises

1. Lie on the floor in a comfortable position with a small book under the head and the legs bent at the knee to avoid a severe curve in the lower back. Place a large book, or better still a brick, on the area of the diaphragm or waistline. Relax either by doing one of the exercises in the relaxation section above, or by simply resting for a few minutes. Notice how as you begin to relax and breathe from the area of the diaphragm, the action of the breath gently pushes the book or brick upwards as it enters the body and begins to fall as the breath leaves the body.

    In this position the shoulders are not involved in the breathing process. As you breath out allow the air to leave the body on a gentle /fff/. Once the air has left the body wait for the body to 'need' a new breath before taking one; if you over-breathe you will feel dizzy. It is important to breathe out at a slower speed than you breathe in. Notice how a rhythm develops. The breath comes in to a count of three or four, there is a slight pause and the breath leaves to a count of four or five. There should also be a pause before the new breath is inhaled.

2. Lying on your stomach, get your head into a comfortable position, most people find lying with the face to one side is best.

Place the book or brick onto the buttocks, so that you can feel it rise and fall as you breathe in and out. This is a useful exercise because it allows you to feel the breath in a way that is impossible when you stand up because you are lying on the abdomen and the action of the diaphragm when breathing in causes displacement of the internal abdominal organs. You are able to feel this as movement in the lower back and buttocks. It is also good for creating a feeling of 'separation' in the lower vertebrae and allowing relaxation in muscles in an area which many of us hold in a state of tension.

3.   Standing in front of a mirror, place one hand on the midriff. As you breathe out, place some pressure on the midriff and notice how the outgoing breath results in the muscles below the hand moving towards the spine. As breath comes into the body the hand will follow the muscles of the midriff outwards. While you are doing this, check in the mirror that the shoulders are not lifting significantly as breath comes in. Begin to develop a more conscious outward breath using /ffff/ to the count of five. Pause and then feel the breath come in under the hand to the count of three, followed by /ffff/ out to the count of five. Once confident with these exercises, increase the duration of the outgoing breath from five to seven or eight. Never force this; what is important is that you become conscious of the fact that the body expands as breath comes in and decreases in size as breath is exhaled.

4.   Stand with your hands stretched outwards in a star position. Breathe out on an /s/ and as you do so bend over to touch the floor, allowing your knees to bend as you go over. Pause until you feel the need to breathe. When you do, stand up and return to your original position and feel the breath re-entering the body as you do so. The object of this exercise is to illustrate that the open body position produces an effortless intake of breath and, when the rib cage is not constricted, breath freely enters the body. This illustrates that a good open posture is a very important aid to good breathing.

Jaw Exercises

The mouth is the only truly moveable resonator and it is important for it to be relaxed and flexible in order for voice and speech to be resonant and free. Any releasing exercises should be done from the 'hinge' of the jaw and not from the front of the mouth.

1. Yawning is an excellent way to release tension in the jaw and pharynx, and the release of tension increases muscularity. Do not stifle yawns, enjoy them.

2. Imagine you are chewing a piece of toffee. Use the whole mouth space and jaw. To avoid this becoming a way of inadvertently increasing tension in the jaw, work with a relaxed, almost slow motion energy that aims to stretch the strap muscles of the jaw.

3. Imagine you have small springs between your molars, which do not allow your teeth to touch, so that the result of attempting to bring the teeth together would be that they spring away from each other. This springing movement also increases the length of the jaw muscles.

4. Place your hands on either side of the face and gently stroke the jaw downwards. Allow the mouth to open as the hands move down the face. Keep the jaw loose, free and mobile.

Exercises for the Articulators

1. Lips need to be exercised in order to keep the muscles capable of making firm explosive sounds. Firstly purse the lips forward and then spread them suddenly into a broad smile. It is important to be aware of the muscles used in the two activities.

2. Curl the upper lip up towards the nose. Curl the lower lip down towards the chin. Purse the lips and then open and close the pursed lips in an action that resembles the mouth of a goldfish.

3. Try balancing a pencil on the upper lip. Blow up the cheeks and then using your fingers 'pop' the cheeks, producing a sound as the air explodes through the lips.

4. Produce an exploding /b/ sound using the lips. Increase this to three /b/s followed by a vowel, e.g. /b/b/bah/. Do the same with /p/ and /p/p/pah/. Follow this with vowels that end on a /b/, for example /oob/ and /ohb/, and with /p/, for example /oop/ and /ohp/.

5. The tongue needs to be exercised so that it is capable of flexible movement without tension. To start, simply stretch the tongue as far out of the mouth as you can and then allow it to relax back into the mouth, leaving the tip touching the lower front teeth.

6. The following exercise aims to stretch the middle of the tongue. Place the tip behind the lower front teeth and then

bunch the middle of the tongue forward and out of the mouth. Hold the stretched position for a few seconds and then release.

7.   Lift the tongue to the ridge behind the upper teeth and explode the consonant sequence /d/d/d/d/ and /t/t/t/t/. Lift the tongue and form an /l/ then precede the /l/ by a series of vowels for example, /eel/ /ool/ /ahl/ /ohl/ /awl/. Use a series of words containing /l/ to exercise the tongue; these can be done with children, asking them to supply the words; for example lorry, land, light, cool, feel, hold, golden. lazy, languid.

Routines

Routine 1 – Floor exercises

1.   *Spine:* Lengthen the spine: imagine you are able to gently separate the vertebrae by moving the head away from the shoulders, the hips from the ribs. Broaden the back by imagining you can widen the shoulder girdle. Gently press the shoulders into the floor then release. Feel that you are longer and broader than you were.

2.   *Jaw and tongue:* Imagine that the jaw hangs off the skull. Feel the space between the teeth. Stretch the tongue out of the mouth, release it and allow it to slip back to a position where it loosely touches the front teeth. Clench the teeth, release and then release a second time. Repeat the exercise three times.

3.   *Scalp:* Release the muscles of the face and scalp. Imagine you are wearing a tennis headband across the forehead. Using the muscles of the face and head, imagine pushing it off the top of the head.

4.   *Neck:* Release the back of the neck by lengthening it. It sometimes helps to push the head gently into the floor, feel the tension, then release it. Gently move the head from the left to the right shoulder. Bring the head back to a central position.

5a. *Breath:* Place one hand on the centre of the body, in the region of the navel. The most extensive breathing activity should ideally happen below the sternum and in the area of the abdomen and lower ribs. Sigh out a feeling of being bored. Notice how the breath returns on its own. Sigh out a feeling of relief, again notice how the breath returns on its own.

5b. Breathing out, notice how the hand sinks down towards the floor. Feel the breath pass over the lips on a gentle /fff/. When you have emptied the lungs, pause and wait until you feel the need for breath. Do not resist it, simply allow the breath to return and notice how the hand on the body rises up towards the ceiling and the lower ribs move upwards and outwards to allow the breath to fill the space below the sternum. The shoulders, neck and upper chest need not be involved.

5c.   Repeat the exercise above breathing out on the sound /sh/. Notice that the breath is used up more quickly on this sound.

5d.   In your head, count to five on an /s/ as you breathe out. Make sure you keep the neck and jaw loose. Do not worry about the quality of the /s/. On the next outgoing breath count in your head to six, and so on. Do not feel that it is important to reach a high number. If you get tense and tight in attempting to do so you have defeated the object of the exercise. Notice that the ribs as well as the muscles under the hand are active in releasing the breath.

5e.   Now feeling very loose (the idea of being drunk helps) turn the outgoing breath into sound and voice the sound /mah/. Build a feeling of vibration in the 'mask' of the face on /mmm/ before opening onto the vowel.

5f.   Do the same using /nah/, /vah/ and /zah/.

5g.   Begin to vary both the pitch and the vowel so that you produce a combination of sounds beginning with /n/, e.g. /noh/, /naw/, /nay/, /now/; do the same using /v/ and /z/.

Routine 2 – Working in a chair

1.   Begin by sitting in an upright chair (such as one commonly used in classrooms). Make sure you find it comfortable. Sit with both 'sitting bones' firmly on the seat. Avoid sitting on one buttock only. Lengthen the spine from the coccyx to the skull. Avoid over-correction and hollowing of the lower back. Feel that the spine is free and flexible. Use the Alexander technique image of a water fountain spouting up through the spine. Let the head be balanced on the top of the spine. Make small movements to the muscles of the neck so as to minimally move the head. No large movements of the head should occur. The feeling to work for is that of the marionette's head, loose but not floppy. Let the jaw feel as if it 'hangs off' the head. Let the tongue feel loose and free in the mouth with the tongue tip touching the lower front teeth.

2. Take the chair and sit back to front on it, so that you can lean over the backrest. This will open up the vertebrae in the lower spine and as long as you release and 'let go' of the shoulders, it is a good position for breathing. You can put your head on your folded arms across the back of the chair.

3. If possible, ask someone to place their thumbs on your spine with their fingers splayed around the lower ribs. This will allow you and them to feel the expansion of the ribs when you breathe in. The movement will result in their thumbs moving away from the spine.

4. Set up a steady rhythm of breathing in and out. Work on breathing in to a count of three and then out to three, then in to a count of three and out to four, and in to three and out to five. As the breath leaves the body, feel it pass between the teeth and lips in a gentle /fff/. Never get competitive and try to get up to a high count, as this leads to breath holding and creates more tension than it releases.

5. On the outgoing breath begin to introduce an effortless /vv/ by simply turning the breathed /fff/ into sound. Feel the vibrations on the lips, teeth and in the mask of the face. If you feel discomfort in the larynx or tension in the back of the neck you are working too hard.

Resonance exercises

We recommend that work on 'opening up' the pharynx is done in conjunction with jaw exercises, so start by trying the following exercises.

1. Keep the lips together with light contact and then try to produce a full yawn or even an attempted or half yawn.

2. Try to imagine chewing gum or toffee which increases in size with every chewing movement. As you do this you will be aware of the increased size and openness of the pharynx.

3. Try an 'inside' smile. In this exercise you relax the lips and 'smile' with the back of the mouth in the area of the oropharynx or where you feel the tonsils might be. The inside smile will increase your awareness of this area and encourage you to open it up.

4. Try and stick your tongue out as far as possible and then try to speak as clearly as possible with your tongue sticking out of your mouth. This is quite difficult to do but you can achieve a certain amount of clarity. It is fun to do and should not be

taken seriously. If you use too much effort you may create more tension than you release, and you may 'gag'. These exercises often result in a need to yawn.

5. Try and create tension deliberately in the jaw, tongue and pharynx and speak a sentence in this very tight way. It is useful to contrast the sound and sensation you have when speaking in this manner with the sound and sensation you have when the sentence is spoken without tension.

6. Contrast the full mellow sound that you achieve with an open relaxed pharynx with that of a tight constricted pharynx which results in a harsh metallic sound.

7. Try to say the sentence 'Eve ate apples all afternoon' with excessively tight cheek muscles, then try it with excessively loose cheek muscles. Try the same sentence with a tight pulled-back tongue, now try it with a forward floppy tongue and finally try the same sentence with a tight clenched jaw and an excessively open one. Monitor the difference in tension in your cheeks, tongue and jaw in the production of these sentences. Also notice that the quality of the voice is altered when levels of tension change.

8. You can try the same combination of movement with these sentences.

    The five parked cars are mine.
    Now I see the fleecy clouds.
    Not hot rolled gold.
    Mark Parker sent a letter to settle the bet.
    Owen ought to go to Orlando.

    Exercises for the pharynx to develop increased pharyngeal resonance are very useful, not only in altering the resonance of the voice, but also in releasing areas of tension in the jaw and tongue.

9. Try to open your mouth as wide as possible and move into a yawn, feeling the increased size between the molars. Try to concentrate on increasing the size at the back rather than the front of the mouth, because if you try too hard to increase space at the front you will create some unwanted tension.

10. From the yawn move into a sigh as you breathe out. Use /ah/ or /aw/ for practice as this will encourage space in the mouth as well as in the pharynx. Your tongue tip should be touching the lower front teeth but should not be pressed against them.

11. Once you have established the yawn, try to sigh out on /oh/ and then say the following sentences keeping the pharynx as relaxed as possible.

I'd only own a gold Opel said Owen.

Over and over and over again.

There is room for improvisation here and pupils can help by making up sentences as well.

Working on the nasal resonators is more difficult as there is less 'room for manoeuvre' here. Some teachers will speak with regional accents that make greater or lesser use of nasal resonance. The importance of working on nasal resonance is to achieve a balance between oral, nasal and pharyngeal resonance.

12. Try the following sounds in sequence:

ng ah /ng ah/ ng oh/ ng oh/ ng ee/ ng ee/

Make sure there is a contrast between the nasal /ng/ and the vowel so that the vowel remains clear and denasal.

13. Try the following sentences, feeling the vibrations produced by the nasal resonance of the nasalised /m/ and /n/ sounds and the open oral resonance of the vowels.

My mother makes marvellous macaroni.

Mavis and Mildred munched on mackerel.

Many more men marry.

Musicians make music merrily.

Nora is a noisy nanny goat.

No naughty children are known here.

Routine 3 – Exercises in connecting resonators

(To be done after Routine 1 or 2, or after doing the Resonance exercises.)

Sliding and gliding

Use the whole body and move whenever possible during these exercises.

1. *Sirening*: Using the sound /n/ (and imitating the noise of a police siren) describe a vocal circle that begins between the shoulder blades and 'slide' the sound over the top of the head and face. Keeping the sound moving, return to the starting point along an imaginary circular trajectory. This should be easy as long as you keep it playful and do not try to push. You will not hurt the voice in this way. The same can be done with the /ng/ sound (in song) and the /m/, /v/ and /z/.

2.   *Slide*: Stretching up onto the toes with hands in the air, allow the spine to bend over, one vertebra at a time, until you are bent over at the waist. As you do so make the sound of a vowel, such as /oo/ /ay/ /aw/ or /ah/. Make the vowel last as long as the journey from the extended stretch to the bent spine. This exercise can be done in reverse, starting the sound on the floor and sliding it upwards. Some people find this direction easier, others find it more difficult. Eventually both will be possible. If you find the onset of the vowel difficult precede it with an /m/.

3.   *Bowling*: Using the arm to bowl, imagine the ball is the sound /m/ and as it leaves your hand lift the sound up and over the space almost in an arc. Open to the vowel /ah/ halfway through the arc and sustain the sound until it 'lands' on the ground. Do this in slow motion so that it blends from the /m/ into the /ah/ smoothly as it arcs through the air.

4a. *Glide from chest to mouth*: Make an /ah/ producing chest resonance. Feel the vibration by placing your hand on your chest. Make an /aw/ being aware of the resonance in the mouth. Notice how the lips form a megaphone shape.

4b. Begin by patting the chest while sounding /mah/ – feel the vibrations. Glide the /ah/ vowel into an /aw/ in the mouth slurring from one sound to another, for example /mah – aw/.

Repeat the exercise beginning with the /aw/ resonating in the mouth and then glide this sound upwards into an /ee/. The glide from the /aw/ to the /ee/ should be relaxed and effortless and the overall balance of one sound moving from one space to another should be maintained. In all these exercises the smooth continuum of sound is worked for and any feeling of pushed or strangulated sounds should be avoided. If a 'crack' in the flow of sound develops, just go slowly back over that area in the range. Using the hand or arm to describe the movement is often an effective aid to developing flexibility of the voice.

5.   *Fire engine/ambulance siren*: Using /ng...ah/ /ng...ah/ /ng...ah/, create the movement between head and chest resonance. This exercise explores the vocal range and extends the extremes of pitch and resonance. The dual-pitch siren is used for different vehicles in different cities, so the title of this exercise may not be correct for everyone, but can be adapted.

6.   *Slurring and singing*: Using a piece of text (just a few lines), slur the voice drunkenly and smoothly through the whole range. Try a line sung to a made-up tune. Speak it to that tune. Reduce the tune but keep the movement in the voice.

It is important to 'play' and not to strive for perfection as this usually results in creating tension rather than releasing it.

Exercises for Onset of the Note

The term 'onset' refers to the approximation of the vocal folds in order to produce sound. The following exercises use /h/ before vowels as during the production of an /h/ the vocal folds do not come together completely and so limit hard attack. Try using the following word list to achieve a gentle onset of the note, initially using /h/ to achieve this and then trying the word without /h/.

h	at	at	h	unusual	unusual
h	it	it	h	under	under
h	eat	eat	h	above	above
h	only	only	h	every	every
h	ill	ill	h	arm	arm

Again it is very worthwhile to encourage your class to join in with these exercises; they can think of word lists as well as short sentences beginning with vowels, for example:

Amy ate an apple.
Arnold's uncle urged him to eat up.
Esther owned an enormous elephant.
Alright Arthur move along immediately.

In the second part of the exercise contrast it with the gentler onset experienced when beginning a word with an /h/.

Happy birthday Harriet.
How are you?
Here's a helping of ham.
Have some angel cake.

Exercises For Primary Classes

Exercises for teacher and pupils

1.   Ask the class to stretch and yawn like a cat, not forgetting to stretch the spine, fingers and toes.

2. Everyone should wrinkle up the face so as to pull the ugliest face possible. Relax. Then smile as widely as possible. Relax.

3. Stretch the tongue out as far as possible as if 'pulling tongues'. Relax.

4. Blow through the lips like a horse in order to loosen the mouth area. Relax.

5. Imagine the class is playing tennis. To begin with, use the sound /b/ as the ball and everyone uses an imaginary tennis racquet to hit the /b/. The first part of the exercise is bouncing the /b/ on the racquet using short staccato sounds. The second part of the exercise is to lengthen the stroke so that the /b/ develops into a /bah/ and travels a distance. The distance should be specified, e.g. 'Let the /bah/ land on the floor at the other end of the line/classroom/hall'. Sometimes these exercises are best done in slow motion. The consonant /d/ can be similarly used and developed into /dah/ for the second part of the exercise.

6. If possible teach the class a nursery rhyme or a few phrases in a foreign language, so as to allow them to take up vocal and verbal positions not encountered in English or in the mother tongue.

Exercises For Secondary Classes

Exercises for teacher and pupils

1. Standing, ask the class to follow you in stretching up through the right-hand side. Take the arm above the head and over to the left side. The greatest extension is felt when the heel of the hand is used in the stretch. Now do the same with the left arm taking it up and then over to the right. Make the class aware of the movement of the rib cage in the stretch.

2. Ask the class to stand as badly as they possibly can. This usually involves standing with the weight on one leg, and the head and shoulders slumping forward. Often the arms will be folded across the chest and generally there will be a reduction of space between the hips and lower ribs, making easy breathing, centred in the diaphragmatic and lower rib area, difficult. The second part of this exercise is to ask them to now correct the posture, so that they draw themselves up and out of the slumped position, re-adjusting their weight so that it is equally distributed across both feet. The spine will be long, the chest open and the head easily balanced on top of the spine. Once

the class know what they are looking for in good alignment, they can take it in turns to stand badly so that a partner can then physically change their posture by moving them into a more open and more aligned posture. This exercise can be done as 'puppets' with quite young children, e.g. A is the puppet, B the puppeteer who re-arranges the puppet's posture.

3.   The class should now divide into pairs, and take it in turns to do the following exercises. The partner who is not doing the exercise has the important task of feeding back information to the partner actively involved in the exercise. Feedback should be about the physicality observed and the level of tension monitored. Partner A stands in front of partner B and tries to release all tension from the shoulder area. Partner B then lifts the shoulder girdle of A and reports on how much, if any, resistance is encountered. Generally A will either hold the shoulders down or assist in raising them. The aim is to do neither, but rather to release the shoulders so that they can be moved by B. This is best achieved by attempting to isolate the shoulders and giving up all control over them. If the shoulders are locked they will be difficult to move; if, however, A is successful in isolating them, B will feel they are heavy but loose. Feedback is very useful here as it begins to raise aware-ness of just how much tension is being held in the shoulder girdle. Change over so that A becomes the monitor and B does the exercise.

4.   Once the shoulders have been released, then a similar exercise is done with the arms. Partner A stands or sits with the arms hanging loosely by the sides. B lifts A's arm as A attempts to fully release the muscles making the arm pliable and flexible and under the control of B. The temptation again is for A to control the arm, particularly when the arm is raised. When the arm is dropped by B it may remain in 'mid-air' illustrating that the muscles retain tension. Change over and repeat, remembering the importance of feedback.

5.   The class should stand, with knees unlocked and spine long. They should become aware of the way in which the head balances on the top of the spine and, releasing the jaw, should gently allow the head to nod in a small 'yes' gesture (up and down) and then in a 'no' gesture from side to side. Movements should be loose but minimal.

6.   Move the head towards the right shoulder and using the nose as a pencil, 'draw' straight lines from floor to ceiling. The

action here should again be one of fluidity and ease rather than of high energy. The muscles of the neck will feel the lengthening effect of the exercise. It is very important that the jaw should not be clenched.

7. In pairs again, A should stand in front of B. B places his or her hands around the lower ribs of A with the thumbs resting on either side of the spine. Beginning with A breathing out, B should notice how much the lower ribs decrease in width as breath is exhaled. The A group should be told to gently wait until they feel the need to breathe and then both A and B should notice how the breath replenishes and how, as it does so, B's hands on A's ribs move outward and the thumbs move away from the spine. Repeat, changing over A and B.

8. Ask the whole class to pat their chests as they release the sound /mah/. They should be encouraged to feel the vibrations in the chest. Imagine the class are drawing the letter /m/. They should use the hand to slowly describe the letter as the voice follows, voicing /mmmmmmm/. They can then describe a circle using /nnnnnnn/ while drawing the circle at the same time. In all these exercises it is important to feel the vibrations rather than listening to the sound.

9. Blow up the cheeks and with the fingers pop them. Blow raspberries. Make the noise of a motorbike to the sound /brmmmm/ and of a speedboat to the sound /vrmmmm/.

10. Using gibberish, ask members of the class to improvise a few lines in a made-up language and let the class repeat it. The object here is not to produce perfect sounds, but to explore a different usage of sound sequences.

11. Select a short passage of text that has energised language and let the class explore this together. Do not worry about analysing meaning, simply encourage exploration and enjoyment in the speaking of the words. Meaning will generally evolve.

A Quick Warm Up, using some of the Exercises already Explored

Some warming up can be done quite inconspicuously in the bus, the car or on the train. For example:

Loosening the body

- Gently push the shoulder blades together and feel the opening of the front of the chest as you do so. Do this three times.

- Lift the shoulders slightly and then release them. Do this three or four times.
- Using two fingers of the right hand gently push the chin into the neck and feel the stretch of the muscles down the back of the neck. Do this three times.
- Imagine that the head is balanced on the top of the spine on a greasy ball-bearing.
- Move the head very smoothly and easily in a nodding 'Yes' motion.

Loosening the jaw

Checking the level of tension in the jaw is always recommended.

- Take the hands up to the cheekbones and gently stroke the jaw downwards allowing the strap muscle to release and lengthen.
- Imagine that the jaw is heavy and let its weight carry the jaw downward. Feel the separation of the teeth. Monitor whether or not the teeth are clenched, if so release the strap muscle.

Breathing out

- Sigh out to the count of five on an /ff/. When you finish the breath in the lungs simply allow them to refill.
- Sigh out to a count of six on an /ss/. Repeat the refill process.
- Sigh out to a count of seven on a /th/. Repeat the refill process.
- Sigh out to a count of eight on a /sh/. Repeat the refill process.

If you are in a private space (the car is ideal, as long as it is not overheated and your shoulders and neck are not locked in a state of tension due to traffic jams) you can begin to voice on the outgoing sigh.

- Sing out to a count of seven on an /mmmmm/.
- Sing out to a count of eight on a /vvvvv/.
- Sing out to a count of nine on a /zzzzz/.

Always be aware of tension in the muscles of the neck when you sound, particularly as you come to the end of the breath capacity.

Moving the voice

- Describe a line from the floor to the ceiling using a trilled /r/. At first you may find that you cannot sustain the line of breath and sound but with practice you soon will.

Vowels

It is important to explore the length of vowels, for example /heat/, /he/ and /heal/ all contain the same vowel /ee/ but depending on the sound that follows the length of the vowel is altered.

- Try this sequence: /mmmm aw/ mmmm oh/ mmmm ee/, sustaining the vowel.
- Feel that the /mmm/ brings the voice forward onto the lips and that the vowels are free, forward and not held in the throat.
- Try working with /h/ in front of the vowels, for example /h-ah/ /h-ay/ h-aw/.

Lips and tongue

- Purse the lips and then circle them: beginning at the right-hand corner of your mouth, take the lips down to your chin and then round to the left-hand corner and then up to the nose and back to the starting point. Reverse the action.
- Repeat the same exercise with the tongue and make sure you stretch it and attempt to describe the full circle. Avoid missing out any section of the circle.

Consonants

When exercising the consonants it is important to feel the muscularity of the sounds. For example /b/ is made with a firm coming together of the lips and then exploded by the breath. /d/ is made by the lifting of the tongue to the teeth ridge and then being exploded by the breath. /f/ is made by the placing of the top teeth on the lower lip and the fricative action of the breath as it passes through. The best way to exercise these sounds is to speak a short passage of verse that includes a plethora of consonants, for example:

Full fathom five thy father lies,
Of his bones are coral made;
Those are the pearls that were his eyes;

Nothing of him that doth fade,
But doth suffer a sea-change
Into something rich and strange.
The Tempest – **William Shakespeare**

This brief warm up can be done in less than ten minutes.

Chapter 11
Suggestions for Volume and Distance

This chapter includes two strategies which proved very useful in our workshops with teachers, and deal with two very commonplace activities that teachers undertake. The first is the need to summon children from a distance or to address students who may be some distance from them. This often leads to the teacher thrusting the head forward and constricting the voice. The second strategy is for 'shouting', which is an activity that many teachers find vocally difficult. We have spoken at length about the importance of posture and head position and the freedom needed in the muscles of the neck and jaw.

The instinctive energies rallied in situations requiring organisation of large groups and involving any element of crowd control or discipline, all work against the idea of the free neck. Many teachers find themselves using pointing and prodding gestures with the fingers and head and when this happens, it is no surprise that not only the voice is lost, but the control of the class goes too.

The value of stillness cannot be emphasised enough (by stillness we mean free, grounded stillness, not rigid, held stillness), not simply the stillness of the individual in the organisational position, but also the quietness and stillness required to allow thinking, and therefore learning, to take place. Status afforded to those who find a quality of quiet control is generally high, and far outweighs that of teachers who expend a great deal of energy in order to achieve the same effect.

There are many misconceptions about making the voice easily audible. Most of these have evolved because the language used to encourage better audibility tends to produce an image of the voice 'pushing' forward. We hear 'Speak up', 'Speak out', 'Throw the voice', 'Project the voice', 'Reach the back of the room', 'Notch up the volume', and even 'Hit them with the sound'. In reality such suggestions only add to the teacher's tension through a misuse of energy. How much better, and of course more appropriate, it would be to suggest that the teacher 'Includes the whole class in the conversation' or 'Shares the information', so concentrating on the intention behind the word and conveying this intention, rather than simply creating more sound.

Some Pointers from Actors

Actors, often excellent communicators off stage as well as on, are not limited to high volume in order to be heard. When an actor is comfortable in a very large space, he or she is able to reduce volume to the minimum without losing clarity. They have learned how effectively resonance gives body and carrying power to the voice, and how, keeping the 'thought' behind the words at all times adds to clear delivery and audibility. Actors use the term 'motivating' for this process. It is very common for the meaning of a phrase to be lost to an audience if the actor has lost concentration of the thought behind the phrase. Likewise the teacher who does not feel a natural enthusiasm for the subject, or who feels coerced into the teaching of a subject he or she would rather not teach, can develop audibility problems because they have limited commitment to the words. Actors also learn through experience that at times it is important to allow space between words and phrases in order to allow them to stand out from the others around them. Physical stillness and a low vocal volume are often used for the most significant of speeches. In addition they are concerned with the energised use of consonants, particularly the final ones that define words. An example of this is the difference between the words 'road', 'rogue', 'roam', 'rose' and 'rope', when spoken. The definition of the last consonant is needed if the word is going to be heard and understood, otherwise confusion can occur when final consonants are ill defined. Speech is made up of voiced and voiceless sounds. In large spaces it is the voiced sounds that carry, because they set up vibrations in the space.

In order to experience this, use the spoken voiced /z/ in the place of the spelt /s/ in the following words and notice the difference the resonance in the voiced sound makes. We do not use these in close conversation but they are necessary in larger space or when speaking to larger groups.

Eyes	ears	hands	faces
has	is	was	his
hers	knees	ideas	calls
pens	roads	seas	easy

Now try:

Friends, Romans, countrymen, lend me your ears;
I come to bury Caesar, not to praise him. *(Julius Caesar, Act 3 sc 2)*

All vowels are voiced and can help the carrying power of the voice but in contemporary speech we tend to undervalue the vowels and do not give them their full length or energy. Some people perceive those who commit fully to vowels to be flamboyant and extrovert, personality traits we shy away from. This is unfortunate because vowels also carry enormous musical and emotional value and if used fully give both resonance and range to the voice, while at the same time increasing carrying power.

Exercise

Take the vowels out of the following words and string them together without the intrusion of any consonants:

How sweet the moonlight sleeps upon this bank! *(Merchant of Venice, Act 5 sc 1)*

When you find the innate musical and emotional value of the vowels you also tap into the larger vocal resonance of the voice. Notice the way the vowel sounds carry, because they are voiced and continuing, they have vocal 'body'. If we can balance speech with more vowel sounds, we immediately develop a great ability to easily fill the space.

In the theatre, what is often considered by audiences as being inaudible is in fact perfectly loud enough. What it lacks, more often than not, is clear intention and definition. These are aspects that teachers can work on and which will improve delivery and therefore audibility immediately. Any teacher working too hard to produce a louder volume is likely to 'lock' breath and neck, thus reducing peripheral vision, raising the pitch and giving an impression of aggression which may lead to a loss of goodwill and attention from the class.

When working with actors it becomes apparent that the loudest volumes (which are not used all that often by actors, and certainly not for prolonged periods) are sustainable with very little effort when they come from a free and open body position. The minute the neck locks, high volume is not an option without causing vocal discomfort. The actor works to find ways of producing volume without 'closing down' the open neck position. Above all the actor fills the space physically and vocally without 'pushing' to reach the back.

Most actors work to develop an omni-directional approach, because so many theatres today are not built with a proscenium arch and often there are audience members behind, as well as in front of them. An actor–audience relationship is not unlike that of the modern teacher who, it is said, 'needs eyes in the back of the head'. This omni-directional approach involves keeping an active level of communication going all the time, developing the peripheral vision, using voice that is resonant and therefore has carrying power, and using defined consonants and receiving as well as emitting energy. In terms of the space itself, it is important to see it being inhabited by the audience as well by the actor or teacher. There should never be an 'us and them' approach, as this is likely to promote a feeling of alienation. Actors usually walk about the space in order to familiarise themselves with it and to find out how their voices behave within the space. Once they have a feel for the natural acoustic of the space they can modify their voice accordingly.

Exercises

There are specific techniques that often prove successful in gaining a centred physical stillness and a vocal quality that is unrestricted by the neck muscles going into the extreme positions of 'fight' or 'flight'. These exercises work because there is a changed attitude in the speaker who, instead of submitting to the urge to reach out, or (in extreme cases) to 'punch' out to the class with the voice, stands their ground and imagines that the voice is beginning at the back of the class room and travelling towards him/her.

The 'Towards Strategy'

Exercises

1. *Moving from the wall:* Find a spot on the wall and, standing a few inches from it, concentrate on voicing the sound /mah/ and placing the sound on the spot. Once you have established this keep concentrating on the spot but slowly move backwards away from the wall. You may find at first that you run out of breath quite quickly, but with practice this will improve and you will find you can move further away without loss of breath. It is important to become aware of the sound being drawn away from the point of concentration and towards yourself. The neck and head never thrust forward and the body

remains 'open'. As you continue to do the exercise, increase the arc of sound so that instead of describing a straight line from the wall to yourself, allow the sound to arc upwards and over towards you. The arc is used because it explores vocal range and in speech we use vocal range all the time.

2.   *Calling*: Imagine you are on a boat or mountain top, and that you are calling to a friend on another boat or mountain top. Neither point of focus is at an uncomfortable distance, but you will need to use an extended sound. Place your hands to your mouth and call in a moderate volume, 'Hello there.' The person pretending to be on the second boat or hill answers, also using the call. If improvisation is a problem, a simple question and answer such as 'How are you?', ' Very well, thank you' can be planned beforehand. The call is best seen as a continuous sound that lifts and arcs from the mouth of the caller to the ear of the receiver. Shouting should never be used for the exercise, which is about sustaining sound and can be done, with practice, with very little volume.

3.   *Attracting attention*: Use the exclamation 'Hey!' in order to attract somebody's attention at the other side of the room. In this exercise it is important to avoid an aggressive approach as in aggressive mode the sound is forced out. The neck and jaw will thrust forward and the habitual laryngeal setting is altered, the larynx is compressed – often accompanied by vocal discomfort. The fists will often clench, and the shoulder girdle will invariably tighten. The knees will generally lock. It is therefore very important to work in a non-aggressive manner.

Try instead to imagine that the starting point of the sounds is from the individual whose attention you are wanting to attract. Instead of pushing the sound out from yourself, draw it towards you. Try using the hands and arms to help you draw the sound slowly over the space until it reaches you. The sound becomes elongated and the vowel is utilised to allow the sound to travel. This allows you to hold your centred physical position. The head need not be thrust forward, in fact you can retain optimum alignment and the neck can remain free, allowing the peripheral vision to be maintained.

4.   *Pick pocket*: Using the image of drawing sound towards yourself over the space, imagine that you are lifting a scarf out of the pocket of a passer-by. Start by standing fairly close to them and saying the phrase, 'The scarf is mine' as you move away from

the passer-by. Elongate the vowels and lift and arc the voice, as if it travelled with the scarf, from the pocket to you.

The second part of the exercise is to start further away from the passer-by and vocally 'hook' the scarf and some money out of the imagined pocket. Use the phrase, 'The money and scarf are mine.' The use of /m/ aids the voice because it is resonant and a continuous consonant. You should experience a feeling of sustaining sound as you did in the calling exercise.

5.   *Fishing exercise*: This is similar to the pick-pocket exercise. Imagine a fishing line that you have already cast. Establish where the line and hook has landed and this will become the focal point for your sound. Take in breath easily and without tension and release it on /mah/ as you reel the line in towards yourself. Once the 'drawing towards' of the line has been established, you can develop the exercise by gently increasing volume as the line travels towards you. As with the other exercises the head and neck should not be thrust outward, but stay in a balanced and unfixed position on the spine while voicing.

The principle of all these exercises is that you draw sound towards yourself and from the point of communication, rather than pushing it out towards the point of communication. This is quite obviously an image and one that goes against physical science, nevertheless it keeps the body aligned and is a great aid in the struggle against the tendency to thrust sound out, locking neck and losing all sense of co-ordinated speech and communication.

Healthy Shouting

We know that it is possible to shout without hurting or damaging the voice. Nevertheless many teachers trace a vocal problem back to an incident when they, frustrated and angry, have shouted at a child or group of children. They feel a catch in the throat, a loss of vocal freedom and experience a need to force the sound out. They feel the result immediately as roughness in the larynx, a hoarse raspy sound or reduced range. They then proceed to attempt to clear the throat but generally to no avail.

Children in the playground, however, seem able to shout, call, yell and even shriek with no problems. They are being playful and therefore they are free of tension. There is often a quality of laughter lurking beneath the shout. If you look at their faces you see the open expression which is also mirrored by the body posture. The head is aligned, the chest open. The sense of fun removes the tension in the upper body, and generally children are running when they shout and the release this action gives to the voice avoids the chance of damage. There are exceptions and some children have to be taught to shout without harming the voice. Actors, too, are often able to produce blood-curdling cries and yells without damage. It must be said that many of them have to work at it, to find a technique that works against the emotion of the moment.

All the calling and 'toward' exercises in this section are important for the development of a 'shout' but here is a work-out designed to assist the process. It is important to warm up the voice before attempting the shouting exercises and to precede them with breathing exercises and exercises which release tension in the larynx. If you begin to experience discomfort, it is a signal to stop the exercises and return to breath support work. It is also vital to have a clear idea of your point of focus, that is, of the individual or groups with whom you wish to communicate. Although the term 'shouting' conjures up ideas of anger, it is always inadvisable to use high volume if you are angry. When you are angry it is very difficult to separate energy and tension, and often 'inexperienced' shouters are not able to use high energy without constriction, especially if they are having to deal with the additional stresses involved in feelings of anger. It is much more effective to use a controlled and supported sound because any indication of anger suggests a loss of control on the part of the speaker and this undermines authority, rather than increasing it. By removing focus from the larynx and using breath support effectively, you can successfully produce a very high volume without hurting the voice. There are other helpful strategies, such as increasing the precision of the articulation and using greater vocal range than normal, which remove the need to resort to excessive volume.

Shouting Work-Out

1. It is important to precede this with work on shoulder, neck and jaw release.
2. Do Exercise 2 in the Breathing section of Chapter 10. This involves lying on your stomach with a weight on the buttocks and breathing down as low in the body as possible. Develop the exercise by imagining that the breath leaves the body via each of the vertebrae until it reaches the mouth. Practise this

using the voiceless /fff/ and then use a gentle /mmm/. Once you have established the journey of the /mmm/ begin it in the coccyx and increase the energy as you travel up the spine, when you approach the shoulder blades open the sound into a vowel, for example /mmm*ah*/. Repeat the exercise using different vowels such as /mmm*aw*/, /mmm*oh*/, /mmm*oo*/. Allow the voice to change pitch and to lift and arc as you release the sound. As long as you 'begin' the sound well below the level of the larynx it is possible to develop considerable volume without restriction.

3. *The yoga cat*: Kneel on all fours, and keep your hands directly below the shoulders. As you breathe in, curve the lower back up towards the ceiling as the head tucks in towards the chest. As you breath out, allow the lower back to sink towards the floor as you imagine the breath moving up through the spine and, as the head comes up and eyes look towards the ceiling, allow the breath to leave the body.

4. After having done this exercise several times on the floor, stand up and vocalise the sound /mmmmmm/ and imagine it is travelling up the spine. As it reaches the shoulder blades, open the sound out into an /ah/. It may be easier to start in a bent-over position and to unfold through the spine as you produce the sound, synchronising the movement with the sound.
    A word of caution: As you release the vowel and lift the eyes upward do not extend the neck so that you restrict the pharynx.

5. Keep working on this exercise and open to a variety of vowels for example: /mmmmmm*aw*/, /mmmmmm*oh*/, /mmmmmm*ay*/.

6. Once you are happy with this begin to build volume, feeling the real release of the vowel. Once again never be tempted to start the sound at the level of the larynx. The secret of 'shout-ing' is to begin the sound well below the level of the throat. By picturing the sound starting in the coccyx you remove the stress from the throat. This is of course an image, but it helps to keep the sound free. At this stage never get louder than is comfortable and keep the exercises in the style of a call.

7. (In pairs) Imagine each of you is on the top of a hill, some distance apart. Partner A cups their hands around the mouth and calls to B, ' Red roses, who will buy?' B responds, 'How much for a dozen?'

When this is well established and tension free, use the follow lines:

A: Ill met by moonlight, proud Titania!

B: What, jealous Oberon?

(*Midsummer Night's Dream, Act 2 sc 1*)

8.   Begin to introduce an attitude of censorship into the dialogue, still keeping the quality of breath support and vocal freedom.

9.   Now try some of the phrases you are likely to use in the teaching situation, e.g., 'Class four, books away, please,' or, 'Close your desks and stand in line please.' Intone the phrase first on one note, then use the hill-calling exercise and thirdly imagine calling it to the group or child in question.

Suggestions for Muscularity

An excellent and enriching way of exercising the muscles of speech is to work on extant material. Tongue twisters are useful and can be fun, but can be ill-advised as they tend to be done without being related to meaning. There is much wonderfully structured and honed verse that offers not just a muscular exercise, but stimulation of the imagination and in addition demands commitment to rhythm and phrasing. The benefits of using verse are numerous as these passages increase vocabulary, stimulate ideas and discussion and offer the experience of speaking out loud and exploring language.

Conclusion

The context in which the exercises and strategies outlined in this book will be applied will be different for each individual depending on the specific vocal demands they encounter. The essential work undertaken by those who choose to teach is reliant on a flexible and free vocal mechanism and on the teacher's ability to convert thoughts and ideas into sounds, words and language. The fact that we take our voices so much for granted and only think about them when they do not work effectively is an indication of the general resilience of the voice and the synchronicity of thought and speech. When a problem does occur it is often as a result of an increase in tension or stress which alters the fine balance that usually exists between the production of voice and the effort levels required to achieve easy and effortless voicing.

   The successful school answers the needs of both the students and staff and therefore raising the awareness of vocal needs amongst teachers, head teachers, governors and those in charge of the education authorities and educational training colleges is of paramount importance.

Voice problems can be successfully treated by specialists in the field of voice and it is important not to sacrifice a career you love because of lack of specialist intervention. The help is out there. Go and get it.

This book will have been productive if through its cocktail of early warning signs, anatomical information, strategies and exercises, it raises awareness of voice in general, promotes good vocal hygiene and helps to steer teachers and professional voice users who are experiencing difficulty towards the help they need and can so easily find.

In industry and commerce the focus is now on investment in staff in order to increase productivity; the focus in education must be on the teachers who deliver it. Many teachers who want to remain within the profession regrettably feel unable to withstand the high levels of stress with which they have to cope, often manifested in their voice problems, and move on to less stressful careers.

It is our hope that this book may provide the necessary support, information and guidance to halt this inexorable process.

Suggested Reading

Atkinson M (1984) Our Masters' Voices. London: Routledge.

Berry C (1973/1994) Voice and the Actor. London: Harrap (1973), Virgin (1994).

Berry C (1975/1994) Your Voice and How to Use it Successfully. London: Harrap (1975), Virgin (1994).

Berry C (1994) The Actor and the Text. London: Virgin.

Boone DR (1991) Is Your Voice Telling on You? London: Whurr.

Bunch M (1992) The Singing Voice. New York: Springer Verlag.

Burniston C (1966) Spoken English in Advanced Education. Southport: English Speaking Board.

Burniston C (1972) Into the Life of Things. Southport: English Speaking Board.

Covey SR (1994) The Seven Habits of Highly Effective People. London: Simon & Schuster.

Gelb M (1981) Body Learning. London: Delilah Books.

Greene M, Mathieson L (1991) The Voice and Its Disorders. London: Whurr.

Linklater K (1976) Freeing the Natural Voice. Drama Book Specialists.

McCallion M (1988) The Voice Book. London: Faber & Faber.

Macdonald G (1994) The Alexander Technique. London: Hodder.

Martin S, Darnley L (1992) The Voice Sourcebook. Bicester: Winslow Press.

Morrison M (1977) Clear Speech. London: A & C Black.

Rodenburg P (1992) The Right to Speak. London: Methuen.

Useful Contacts

Society of Teachers of the Alexander Technique
20 London House
266 Fulham Road
London SW10 9EL

The Society of Teachers of Speech and Drama
The Secretary
Mrs Ann Jones
73 Berry Hill Road
Mansfield
Notts. NG18 4RU

The British Voice Association
77B Abbey Road
London NW8 0AE

The Royal College of Speech and Language Therapists
7 Bath Place
Rivington Street
London EC2A 3DR

Voice Care Network UK
Co-ordinator: Roz Comins
29 Southbank Road
Kenilworth, Warwicks CV8 1LA

The English Speaking Union
36 Charles Street
London WC1

THEATRE EDUCATION DEPARTMENTS

RSC Education Department
Waterside
Stratford-upon-Avon
Warwicks CV36 6BB

The Education Department
The Royal National Theatre
Upper Ground
South Bank
London SE1 9PX

Globe Theatre
New Globe Walk
Bankside
London

The English National Opera
Education Department
St Martin's Lane
London WC2N 4ES

BBC Education Information Unit
White City
London
W12 7TS

British Performing Arts Medicine Trust
18 Ogle Street
London W1P 7LG

References

Atkinson M (1984) Our Masters' Voices. London: Routledge.

Berry C (1992) Shakespeare Comes to Broadmoor. In M Cox (Ed) That Secret Voice. London: Jessica Kingsley.

Berry C (1993) The Actor and the Text. Virgin.

Brown GA (1979) Learning from Lectures. University of Nottingham.

Brown GA (1980) 'Explaining': Studies from the Higher Education Context. Final Reprot to SRRC. University of Nottingham.

Brown GA (1986) Explaining. In O Hargie (Ed) A Handbook of Communication Skills. London: Croom Helm.

Brown GA, Armstrong S (1984) On Explaining. In EC Wragg (Ed) Classroom Teaching Skills. London: Croom Helm.

Brown GA, Hatton N (1982) Explaining and Explanations. London: Macmillan.

Dunkin MJ, Biddle BJ (1974) The Study of Teaching. New York: Holt Rinehart & Winston.

Farb P (1973) Word Play. London: Cape.

Flanders NA (1970) Analysing Teaching Behaviour. New York: Addison Wesley.

Hann J (1979) The Family Scientist. London: Macdonald & Janes.

Hart W (1934) Teachers and Teaching. London: Macmillan.

Honey J (1989) Does Accent Matter? London: Faber & Faber.

Jackson PW (1968) Life in Classrooms. New York: Holt Rinehart & Winston.

Luchsinger R, Arnold GE (1965) Voice Speech Language. London: Constable.

Macdonald G (1994) The Alexander Technique. London: Hodder.

Martin S (1994) Voice Care and Development for Teachers: Survey Report. Voice 3 92–98.

Masuda T, Ikeda Y, Manako H, Komiyana S (1993) Analysis of vocal abuse: fluctuations in phonation time and intensity in four groups of speakers. Acta Otolaryngology 113:4 547–552.

Mehrabian A (1972) Nonverbal communication. Chicago: Aldine.

Rogers C (1975) A Way of Being. Boston: Houghton Mifflin.

Schriffen D (1984) 'Jewish Argument as Sociability'. Language in Society 13:3 311–335.

Schonell FJ, Roe E, Middleton IG (1962) Promise and Performance. University of Queensland Press.

Tannen D (1991) You Just Don't Understand. London: Virago.

Verdolini-Marston K, Sandage M, Titze IR (1994) Effect of Hydration Treatments on Laryngeal Nodules and Polyps and Related Voice Measures. Journal of Voice 8:1 30–47.

Index

swimming baths, 6, 95, 114–115
syllabus changes, 25

tambourines, 93, 115
Tannen, Deborah, 22
tea, 15, 95
technology, 77–78
theatre companies, 79–80, 109
theatres in-the-round, 109, 110
thespians, *see* actors
thoracic vertebrae, 36
throat clearing, 98
throat lozenges and pastilles, 98
thyroarytenoid muscles, 43
thyroid cartilage, 42
time management, 30–31
'tip of the tongue' syndrome, 25
tiredness, vocal, 12, 14
Titze, I.R., 96
toast-masters, 80
tongue
    exercises, 129–130
    warming up, 141
tongue twisters, 151
tour guide, teacher as, 119
towards strategy, 146–148
trachea, 37, 38, 42
trades unions, 21
training
    teacher, 1–2
        stress, 30
    vocal, 5, 11–12

United States of America, 8
University of Gothenburg, 8
upper respiratory tract, 37, 38
    infection, 26, 96–97
urine colour, and hydration level, 95

varnishes, 95
ventilation, 94–95, 101
Verdolini-Marston, K., 96
verse, 82–83, 151

vertebrae, spinal, 36, 48
video use for posture correction, 55–56
violence and frustration, 84
vitamin B, 95
vocal folds, 43–44
    ageing, effects of, 45, 46
    and arytenoid cartilages, 43
    aspirin, effects of, 98
    coughing, 98
    hard attack, 97
    hoarseness, 14, 15, 16
    hormonal effects, 44–45
    hydration, 95, 96
    length, 41
    mechanics of voice, 36, 37
    repetitive stain injury (RSI), 7
    vomiting, effects of, 97
vocal requirements for teaching, 2–3
voice box, *see* larynx
Voice Care Network, 8, 155
voice care provision, 7–9
voice loss, 7, 8, 9
    gender differences, 11
volume, 103, 143–151
    self-monitoring, 93
vomiting, 97

walking, 99
warming up, 99–100, 139–142
warning signals, 12–13, 87–88
water, 15, 95, 98, 114–115
weather conditions, 6, 113, 114
Welsh accent, 68–69
whistles, 114
wind, 114
women, *see* gender issues
work factors, 22
writing position, 92

yawning, 129
yoga, 99
yoga cat exercise, 150